CROWN HIM KING

This book was made possible by:
Pecos Valley Baptist Association
PO Box 267
Artesia, NM 88211

In appreciation of Dr. Claude W. Cone

0-8054-2762-7

Published by Broadman & Holman Publishers,
Nashville, Tennessee

Dewey Decimal Classification: 248.84
Subject Heading: CHRISTIAN LIFE \ JESUS
CHRIST—LORDSHIP

1 2 3 4 5 6 7 8 9 10 07 06 05 04 03

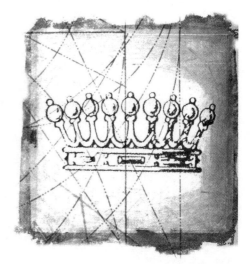

CROWN HIM KING
You Can Empower Kingdom Growth

JAMES MERRITT

BROADMAN
&HOLMAN
PUBLISHERS

NASHVILLE, TENNESSEE

*I dedicate this book to the people
who make up the Southern Baptist Convention,
with whom I look forward to spending eternity
in the kingdom of God in a forever fellowship
with the Church of the Ages under the lordship
of our matchless Savior, Jesus Christ.*

CONTENTS

FOREWORD

This compelling volume by James Merritt presents a clear vision of the most important theme in history: the kingdom of God. There is no grander topic or more significant subject. The kingdom of God is what life is all about! Right now, all around the world, God is building a family of redeemed people who will live, serve, and reign with him for eternity.

The kingdom of God was always uppermost in the mind of Jesus. It was his favorite subject to talk about, and he mentioned it 157 times. In fact, during his ministry Jesus spoke more about the kingdom of God than about any other subject. Unfortunately, theologians and Bible scholars have often made the kingdom of God a dark mystery to most people. Their complex language and esoteric debates about the kingdom's location, timing, and meaning have confused the issue and caused people to avoid this subject. Most Christians are familiar with the phrase "kingdom of God" but can't define it.

Now, in one practical chapter after another, James Merritt unpacks what it *really* means to make Jesus the King, or Lord, of your life on a daily basis. He not only explains the reasons for the kingdom of God (*what* and *why*); he also shows, in simple terms and illustrations, exactly *how* we are to "seek first the kingdom of God." This is a great book to read yourself, then give to a friend who wants to understand what the Christian life is all about.

Don't be surprised when you find yourself pausing to worship God repeatedly as you read this book. When you fully understand God's plan for eternity and your role in it, you cannot keep yourself from bursting out in praise and thanksgiving to our amazing Creator and Savior. History is His Story—from beginning to end!

Forgive me for adding this personal note, but I must admit how much I admire and respect the author. James Merritt is a pastor's pastor, completely dedicated to loving and serving the church, the Bride of Christ. For years he has built a model congregation at First Baptist Church, Snellville, Georgia, that has inspired congregations all across America. I am honored to call him my friend. Because I've seen his life and ministry up close, I recommend this book without reservation. God bless you.

RICK WARREN
Author of *The Purpose Driven Life*
and *The Purpose Driven Church*

ACKNOWLEDGMENTS

I want to acknowledge several people who aided me in the writing of this book.

Lawrence Kimbrough: my editor with whom it was an absolute joy to work; you continually amazed me with your creativity!

Gary Terashita: thanks for your encouragement in believing this could be done and done well.

Broadman & Holman: for being willing to publish this work to begin with!

My church, the Fellowship of Joy: for allowing me to be your pastor and work on projects like this.

My wife Teresa and my sons James, Jonathan, and Joshua: the love of my life and my pride and joy. I am begging one of you to get married soon and give us some grandchildren!

My sweet mother, Miriam: who taught me by example and precept some of the basic principles found in this book.

My Lord and Savior Jesus Christ: for inviting me into his kingdom and making me a kingdom subject. My greatest joy is when I really submit to his lordship and his leadership.

CHAPTER 1

THEY KNOW WHO WEARS THE CROWN

An Introduction

I want to introduce you to some people.

If you saw them on the street, you probably wouldn't pay them any special attention. Though they don't carry their importance around on their sleeves, they are important in all the right kinds of ways— because they understand something important.

They know that *Christ is King.*

❖ ❖ ❖

Kurt and Mattie met each other at a Christian fellowship while in college—she in her second year, he in his third. I don't think you'd call it love at first sight (they were both too serious about themselves to be shopping for mates at the time), but the sparks soon started. Because they attended different churches and were traveling on two different tracks of study, their usual routines didn't place them naturally in each other's orbits. Within a few months after their first encounter, however, Kurt was deliberately circling himself in Mattie's direction in a not-too-unnoticeable attempt to collide with her in the midst of a school day.

Before long, they were dating. But as a rule, it wasn't the usual movies and milk shakes. Theirs was a romance built on getting to know each other not merely through sentiment but through serving God together. They were both deeply involved in ministry—volunteering at a nearby outreach program for troubled teens, as well as getting up early one Saturday a month to teach the Bible to a handful of international students.

Of course they both knew they were at school to study (unlike some people, unfortunately, who rank schoolwork well down on the list of reasons for going to college). His business classes required a lot of extra reading and research, while her music emphasis demanded much practice time, many weekends, and numerous nights in the recital hall.

Still, young love can't stay huddled over the books forever. Neither did theirs. Like any couple growing deeper in love by the day, they faced the almost unavoidable temptations to let their attraction draw them deeper into each other's arms than they knew was right.

But following Christ wasn't a sideline with Kurt and Mattie. Leaving him behind while they went out on Friday night wasn't an option. Yes, they could have easily given in. Even good kids do. But they loved their Lord down into their souls—too much to offend his holiness by letting their thoughts linger too long on the emotions that warmed their hearts but (which they knew) had the potential to scorch and burn.

So they stayed true to their Savior. They committed their innocence into one another's keeping. They didn't merely grin and bear it; they discovered that when one's passion is to please Christ, he can turn any season of waiting into a powerful walk with the Father.

One Saturday afternoon, in a sun-streaked sanctuary, Kurt and Mattie looked into each other's eyes and vowed that only death could separate the love they shared. They entered into marriage with their purity intact—not just in the most technical of ways but in the full liberty of promises kept. They freely became husband and wife without the drain of regrets and secrets—a gift given only to those who have put Christ first, who have sought his kingdom, who have submitted to his will.

Ask Kurt and Mattie if crowning him King was in their best interests or not.

❖ ❖ ❖

Wallace, on the other hand, is not exactly a candidate for romance at his stage of the game. In fact, when his wife of fifty-four years died three summers ago, leaving him an eighty-one-year-old widower, he knew he was on his own for good.

Of course, her death hit hard. For weeks, even months, he labored to smile, to go to Sunday school, to cook his own breakfasts. If you had asked him what he really wanted during those traumatic new days of loneliness and loss, he probably would have told you he wished he could die. No one would have faulted him for choosing to quit. He had lived long and faithfully. He had done his share. He had been delivered a blow that only those who've been there could come close to understanding.

But one night, sitting alone at home, a blanket up to his waist, the television becoming an annoying companion, he realized that in his grief he was putting crowns on the heads of some despicable characters: despair, defeat, self-pity.

And Wallace—good old salt-of-the-earth Wallace— decided he wanted to put those crowns back where they belonged.

He snapped off the TV, leaned over to pick up his well-worn Bible, turned to a passage he had underlined one morning while sitting next to his wife in church, and read again that "all things work together for the good of those who love God: those who are called according to His purpose" (Rom. 8:28).

With tears in his eyes, with the mantle clock ticking loudly in the living room, Wallace spoke the following words out loud: "I'm hurting, Lord. You know that. But, Lord, I do love you. I know you have called me according to your purpose. And if you can use this eighty-five-year-old man to do anything for you, I'm offering myself to you again."

The crown was back in its rightful place.

Soon, Wallace was taking first-aid classes and CPR training and was volunteering with a disaster relief ministry that traveled to hurting regions of the country to help meet the needs of people in crisis. He rejoined the prayer team he and his wife had been part of for years, visiting prospects and committing church members' birthdays to a notebook he kept by his bedside so he could pray for them by name.

The Lord did finally receive Wallace one day— peacefully, in his sleep—but not before he had regained a lifelong calling to the service of Christ's kingdom, not before he had devoted himself anew to his church, not before he had discovered that the life he had surrendered to his Lord had been returned brimming over with meaning and purpose.

A life of total surrender—how totally victorious!

❖ ❖ ❖

Carter is a guy much like Wallace two generations ago. His trade is carpentry, like Wallace's was. And while Carter may not be the fastest worker in the business, his trademark is excellence. In his twenty-year career, he's done everything from framing houses to remodeling kitchens. Nothing seems too hard for him; he can turn the most mundane job into a work of art.

But while the folks at church and down the street enjoy having someone like Carter to answer their carpentry questions and bounce ideas off of—and he's always happy to oblige—he has a lot more than woodworking to talk about.

You see, he learned early in life that God hadn't given him his craft simply to put bread on his family's table. God had given him a talent that put him in people's homes and lives on a regular basis. God had prepared him for a profession that meant spending hours chewing the fat with painters, plumbers, and electricians who might be on the same job site with him for weeks and months at a time. God had placed him in settings where he could not only be known as Carter the carpenter but as Carter the Christian, serving the Master Carpenter.

That's why you're liable to see him at the funeral home, visiting one of the subcontractors he first met a year or so ago—a man who looks painfully uncomfortable and out of place there in his coat and tie—a man whose brother died of a heart attack night before last. Carter knew this, you see, because the man felt comfortable telling him. He knew Carter really cared. That's because Carter doesn't spend the day telling the other guys to quit smoking and swearing; he just whistles his favorite hymns while he works, and watches for opportunities to show them what Christianity looks like in work clothes.

He listens. He lingers. He learns more about the other men over a conversation around their lunch buckets than most people could learn on a weekend fishing trip (though he's even done that with some of them before). Carter is there on purpose. On a mission. He has given his work life over to God. He has found that seeking the kingdom can happen in places where the windows aren't made of stained glass and where the radio blares country songs about men and women who do things they shouldn't.

He has given God the freedom to do anything he wants with this small-town carpenter.

Carter has crowned Jesus as King—where everyone can see it.

❖ ❖ ❖

Jen's work requires a fair share of craftsmanship as well. She's building character into her children's lives.

Jen is a stay-at-home mom—one who hung her

6

professional-looking pantsuits in the closet and traded them in on sneakers and sweatpants. She now spends most of her days making peanut butter sandwiches, reading storybooks, and cleaning up milk spills—that is, when she's not carting someone to ball practice or ballet rehearsal.

It's a tough job. Clothes have to be washed and folded, fevers have to be treated, buttons have to be sewed on. Adult conversation is a rarity. And her preacher's admonition that people need to be doing more at church—when she already helps in children's choir and hosts a small-group Bible study for other moms on Thursday mornings—makes her feel guilty, even though she knows there's not a spare minute for one more thing in her life.

But one morning when the ladies were sharing these same concerns over coffee at Jen's house, the Lord inspired her with a thought that seemed revolutionary to her:

"You know, I think it's great that our pastor challenges us to do more and to be more. I need to hear that. All of us need to hear that. I mean, I'm certainly not above being protective of my time—even selfish with it, on occasion. But God is helping me see that our church is a body of many people at different stages of life, with different gifts and abilities, with different ways of serving. And so I don't have to feel as though anything that needs doing at church is necessarily mine to commit to. I love our church—I really do—and I believe that God does want me to serve him there beyond what I can just do conveniently. But at this stage in my life, raising my children is his calling for me."

Heads nodded. Audible yeses came from every corner.

"I guess I'm starting to see that the various parts of our lives are not really distinct from each other in God's eyes. It's not as though our church life has to exist in isolation from our family life. I believe that when I'm training my children here at home to love God, to know the Scriptures, and to surrender their lives to him for whatever he desires, I'm serving my church at the same time, just like when I'm leading the kids' choir or preparing Christmas baskets for the shut-ins. It's all wrapped up together in being obedient to Christ. He is not just the Lord over my church life but over all of my life."

Another voice joined in. "You know, another part of that, Jen, is that if we're willing to say that we're putting our whole lives into God's hands, then we also have to be willing to say to God: 'I'm willing to put my *children's* lives into your hands as well.' And that can be a pretty scary thought! Do I really mean that I want God's plans for my children to have preference over mine? Could I be OK with seeing the Lord take them across the country or to a foreign mission field, if that was his will for them? I may be willing to pay the cost of Christian discipleship for myself, but am I willing to sit by and watch what it might cost my kids?"

Jen and her friends are grappling with important issues. They are getting the point that belief in Christ is indeed costly to fleshly desires, yet it's the only way to find the peace of absolute surrender. They're understanding that they are allowed to let the high calling of raising their children outrank the many other good things they could be doing out of guilt or for whatever selfish reason.

They are crowning him King, and finding that submitting to Christ and seeing life through kingdom lenses can make an eternal difference.

✢ ✢ ✢

Finally, I'd like you to meet Ronald. He is on staff at a medium-sized suburban church. He was raised in a Christian home, went to a Christian college, earned his seminary degree, and is now putting it to good use as a professional minister—just the way they draw it up on the blackboard.

But Ronald is more than a textbook case for full-time Christian service. He has a deep compassion and calling for the lost that takes him far beyond the boundaries of his job description.

If he wanted to, he could easily occupy himself twenty-four hours a day with ministerial gatherings, committee meetings, and other work-related functions. The daily requirements of his job don't necessarily force him into non-Christian company. But Ronald, like many others who reside in Christian vocations, makes sure that his witness is an ever-present companion in every aspect of his life. If the lost won't come to him, he'll go out and find them.

Rarely does he come home from even the bank or the drugstore without having made some kind of contact with a cashier or a fellow who's filling his gas tank on the other side of the pump or a man waiting in the express lane with him at the grocery. Ronald is a walking, talking testimony of Christ's grace, love, and mercy who is constantly on the lookout for someone who might need a good word. Or an unexpected question. Or a pointed remark that could open the door for him to hear their heart.

Lots of people are amazed by what Ronald can do in the area of personal evangelism. He has so many Bible verses committed to memory, takes so many risks at being rejected, and is so sharp with his reasoned responses to people's objections it is truly inspiring just to watch him operate. Some folks probably think he takes things a little too far. Others hold him up on a pedestal as a person they wish they could be. But one thing's for sure: everyone who has ever met Ronald has been deeply impacted by him.

But does he go around bragging about what God does through his life? Does he act as if he's a little more special to Christ because of the number of people who have been saved through his witness?

He knows that the only one doing the saving around here is his loving Lord. He knows that when he sees an opening to insert Jesus into a conversation, the Holy Spirit is the one putting the ideas in his head and the words in his mouth. When he gets to heaven, there may be a star or two in Ronald's crown for all the faithfulness he's shown, but the only crown that interests him is the one that rests on the head of Jesus. Ron would hate to think what his life would be like if he had kept that crown to himself.

❖ ❖ ❖

The names I've just listed are ones I made up. In fact, I didn't really have any particular individuals in mind when I described these five people. They are actually *composites* of people I have had the privilege of knowing over the years.

These case-study examples of true-to-life Christians—men and women who understand that Christ is King, that he is in charge, that he is not only their Savior but is also their Lord—help us to see what our Christian lives can look like.

It will look different in your life than it does in mine. It may well look different for you now than it did ten, twenty, thirty years ago. But no matter what shape and form the Christian life takes in your experience, if it is lived under the lordship of Christ, it will be filled with the joy of walking in his will.

It works like this:

My first allegiance is to the Lord Jesus Christ. I only want what he wants. I am devoted to the things that are of most importance to him, as they are clearly and broadly expressed through his Word. I have surrendered everything that makes up my life into his keeping. He is in control. He rules, not I.

Now, if my eyes are on any other thing than surrendering to Christ, I will sooner or later find myself far afield from his will, awash in selfish ambition or lazily indifferent to his rightful demands on my life. It is an awful place to be, as every one of us can attest.

But when I am truly being led by the Lord Jesus Christ, I am assured of three things:

1. What I am doing will be best for his kingdom.
2. What I am doing will be best for his church.
3. And however it may appear at the time, what I am doing will also be best for me.

Put another way, there is an eternal order in life, a hierarchy of values that—if followed—will make sure that I see this world as God would have me see it and live my life as God would have me live it.

It looks like this:

Christ
↓
Kingdom
↓
Church
↓
Me

I recently presented these simple, foundational ideas through a series of sermons I preached at our church, and I was humbled by the impact they had— not only in the lives of our church members but also in the lives of those who are reached through our television ministry.

There's nothing all that mysterious about these concepts; the church has been preaching them for generations. But something about the pace and plurality of modern society causes this message to stand in stark contrast to the way many people live today. In an age when we can control many aspects of our lives—when news and information is so near at hand, when packages can be zipped across the country overnight, when pizza can be ordered from our cars on the way home from work— our need for Christ's control over our lives is not as readily evident as it once was.

Maybe that's why we need to hear this again—to be reminded that Jesus Christ is Lord, that his kingdom is eternal, and that even on our best days, we still don't have our own best interests at heart. Only Jesus knows what is best for us in any situation.

I offer this book to you as a biblical model of what can happen when God's people submit to him with their whole hearts. I offer this to you as a means of uniting your church in discovering your place in the work of the kingdom. I offer this with the assurance that you can effect and empower kingdom growth in your corner of the world—right where you live and wherever God may take you.

Are you ready to take back the crowns that you have placed at the feet of such pretenders as money, pleasure, possessions, success, familiarity, comfort, jealousy, and power? Have you had enough of being frustrated in your walk with Christ, shooting yourself in the foot by trying to do it in your own strength? Will you join me in laying down all your plans before the throne of God and opening your empty hands for him to fill with whatever he wants you to do?

At the end of this book, I've included a brief study guide that I hope will be helpful to you in your devotional time or in a small group—as a practical way for you and your church to begin preparing for the specific ways God will use you as you continually submit to his lordship.

May you be blessed as you read and study. May God be honored in all that we do. May his name be exalted; his church, expectant; and his kingdom, empowered through us, his people.

CHAPTER 2

THE KING AND HIS THRONE

Living a Christ-Centered Life

Four last words.

If that's all you had to leave with your wife, your husband, your children, your family, what would they be? "I love you so"?

Four words.

If that's all you were able to say to a dear friend whom you were seeing for the last time, how would you close the book on the years, on all the precious time you'd spent together? "Thank you for everything"?

Four words.

If you could step to a microphone and somehow address every person in the whole world, but you were only allowed the time to deliver a startlingly short sentence, what would it be? What would you say? "I need some water"?

Four words.

With twenty-six letters to choose from, multiplied into a countless number of combinations, yet with almost everything having already been said before, which four words would you choose to string together when those four words had to say everything?

I can tell you *one* thing: According to the Bible, the day is coming when everyone's vocabulary is going to be reduced to just four words (and three of the words have but one syllable). These words will sum up what many have lived their whole lives for; yet, sadly they will be what many have had to die to admit. At the appointed time, however, it will simply be all there is to say.

"Jesus Christ is Lord."

The most powerful four words on earth. The most powerful four words in history. The most powerful four words in time. The most powerful four words in eternity.

That's why in the fleeting moments beside a dying loved one's bedside, these four words can absorb the silence in a room filled with sadness and memories, widening the walls that seem to confine us to our grief, transforming the hard knot of heartache into a glowing thread that connects the sense of loss with a surer sense of eternity.

"Jesus Christ is Lord."

Amid the joy and laughter of human relationships, amid the shared stories and remembrances that unite us with others, amid life experiences that can run the gamut between sheer delight and shocked disappointment, these four words can keep us from being solely dependent on earthly happiness, bored with earthly routine, or defeated and depressed by earthly pain.

"Jesus Christ is Lord."

And while the world seems intent on worshiping its sources of instant gratification, crafting its idols at the ball field and the box office, pursuing pleasure toward a shadowy destination that's always moving and just beyond reach, the profound reality described in these four simple words quakes beneath the loose foundation of modern-day life—extending the Father's warning to those who refuse to relinquish their personal freedoms, yet liberating those who simply believe what already is.

JESUS CHRIST IS LORD
How can four words say so much?

JESUS

We'll start with Jesus. Through the miraculous birth of Jesus of Nazareth, God became a man—so much of a man, in fact, that he gave himself a human name. Stooping lower than we can even begin to imagine, he assumed our own form and nature, descending from a height of exalted splendor where he bore a name "that no one knows except Himself" (Rev. 19:12). Yet out of his great love for us, he dipped into the bank of human names—the Charlies, the Sams, and the Richards—to choose for himself a name that wouldn't sound out of place on the street, in the marketplace, or along the seashore. He would go by a name that Hebrew fathers and mothers had been naming their little boys for generations, and he would live with the same pressures and temptations they faced in their daily lives.

The name itself—Jesus—means "Jehovah saves." It's easy to see, then, that it was a name chosen on purpose—the name given to Joseph by the angel of the Lord: "You are to name Him Jesus, because He will save

His people from their sins" (Matt. 1:21). Otherwise, he could not save. Unless he had been a man, he would not have earned the right to be our mediator, to stand between sinful man and holy God and join the two together across the yawning chasm of sin and death. "For there is one God and one mediator between God and man, a man, Christ Jesus" (1 Tim. 2:5).

Because he is *Jesus*, the price of our sins has been paid through the only way possible—a human being who lived a sinless life, perfectly fulfilling the high demands of God's law.

JESUS CHRIST

His accompanying name—Christ—literally means "anointed one." He is the chosen one, the Messiah, "the Lamb slain from the foundation of the world" (Rev. 13:8 NKJV). The Jesus of the New Testament is the Messiah of the Old Testament, the one who was to come and deliver his people from the hand of the enemy.

And now he has done it. The enemy was not Rome, as many suspected, nor any of the surrounding nations and cultures that even today gnash their teeth at the Jewish people. The enemy to be conquered was not a despot but death. Not a government but the grave. Not holocaust but hopelessness. Not soldiers but sin. In the face of war and hate and terror, no foe in any age *has* ever, *can* ever, or *will* ever be able to take back the ground that Christ has won *for*ever—the fear of hell, the sting of death.

This Jesus is the *Christ*, our Messiah, God's anointed one.

CHRIST THE LORD

But while Jesus is his human name and Christ is his holy name, *Lord* is his heavenly name. Jesus Christ *is* Lord. This means

- he is our Master—therefore, we are his slaves;
- he is our Sovereign—therefore, we are his subordinates;
- he is our Ruler—therefore, we are his servants.;
- he is our King—therefore, we are his subjects.

This is not a choice we make or an option we consider. This is not up for discussion or waiting for a show of hands. *This is the way it is.* Jesus Christ is Lord whether some of us like it or not, understand it or not, believe it or not, accept it or not.

The question, therefore, is not "Is Jesus Christ Lord?" The question of his lordship has already been asked and answered for all eternity, confirmed beyond the shadow of a doubt before any of us were even born. As Peter said to the thousands gathered in Jerusalem on the day of Pentecost: "Let all the house of Israel know assuredly that God has made this Jesus, whom you crucified, both Lord and Christ" (Acts 2:36 NKJV). Jesus himself attested to this when speaking to his disciples: "You call Me Teacher and Lord. This is well said, for I am" (John 13:13). The question of his lordship is an established fact. Period.

But the question that still remains for men and women living in the twenty-first century, the question you and I must answer at some point during our journey through life, is this:

"Is Jesus Christ *my* Lord?"

Being Lord, you see, is something only *he* can do, but *acknowledging* his lordship is something *you* must do. That's why our answer to this question has such huge ramifications:

- It determines our spiritual relationship with Christ, either assuring or placing into doubt whether we are saved.
- It reveals the extent to which we value Christ's personal ownership of our lives, either recognizing or rejecting his rightful position over us.
- It affects how we use our time and resources, either confirming or dismissing his say-so over our actions and decisions.
- And it determines our eternal destiny, either identifying or disqualifying us as one of God's people.

Let me assure you that Jesus is not satisfied with simply having a place in our lives. He doesn't want to be just a part of our plan, point B or C on our calendar, or one factor among others in our overall list of priorities. He doesn't want prominence in comparison with other things in our lives; he wants *preeminence* over everything in our lives.

Why?

Because in fully surrendering to him, we align ourselves with the reality of who he is, our lives fall into proper order under the rule and reign of his kingdom, and we find in serving him the only true freedom that can be known and experienced this side of heaven.

Until he is our Lord, he is not our Savior.

JESUS' LORDSHIP DETERMINES OUR SPIRITUAL RELATIONSHIP

Why did Jesus die?

Why was he raised from the dead?

Why is he alive and reigning this very minute on the throne of the universe?

To save us from our sins, right?

I'll admit, that's a great answer. It's true that the result of these glorious acts in Christ's life have resulted in our full and total forgiveness from the sin that could have easily kept us separated from God from now into eternity. But the Bible gives us a better, more thorough answer: "Christ died and came to life for this: that He might rule over [be *Lord* of] both the dead and the living" (Rom. 14:9).

Do you see the difference, the deeper truth at work here? Jesus didn't just die to cleanse us from our sins, to be our Savior. If that were the case, we would only have needed to turn our attention to him for a moment, to shake hands on the deal and tell him we'll look forward to seeing him in heaven. The cameras flash, the lights go down, and we all go home in a better mood.

But God is aware that we need more than that. *Jesus* is more than that. He has not come to us like a rich uncle, sweeping into town for an overnight visit, unpacking a case of gifts from his fancy car before hurrying off the next morning on a pressing engagement. Christ has come to us *to stay.* To live. To take up residence on the throne of our hearts, just as he dwells already on the throne of heaven.

He *has* come with a gift but not a gift that is somehow detached from who he is, one that separates his saving grace from his lordship. The gift is *himself*—the gift of remaining with us forever in a spiritual relationship where we are the servants and he is the Lord. "For we are not proclaiming ourselves but Jesus Christ as Lord, and ourselves as your slaves because of Jesus" (2 Cor. 4:5).

Watch this transformation happen in the life of Paul: When Jesus met him in a stream of holy, blinding light on the Damascus Road, Paul asked two questions, one after the other:

- The first question was, "Who are you, Lord?"
- When Christ's answer came easily to that question, Paul asked the next one—the natural one, the logical one, the only one for those who have truly looked into the face of Christ and seen him for who he really is: "Lord, what do you want me to do?" (Acts 9:5–6).

Paul recognized Jesus as Lord, and he responded by submitting to his lordship. Had he rejected Christ as his Lord, he would also have been rejecting him as his Savior.

Savior *and* Lord?

Does this seem as if God is asking too much of us? Does this sound foreign to what we have always believed, as though he were adding a second layer of steps to the gift of salvation?

- Not if you believe: "If you confess with your mouth, 'Jesus is *Lord*,' and believe in your heart that God raised Him from the dead, you will be saved" (Rom. 10:9, emphasis added).
- Not if Paul was right in instructing the Colossians: "Therefore as you have received Christ Jesus the

21

> *Lord*, walk in Him, rooted and built up in Him and established in the faith, just as you were taught" (Col. 2:6–7, emphasis added).

- Not if you are convinced that the angels received specific orders from God to proclaim to the shepherds from a starlit sky: "Today in the city of David was born for you a Savior, who is Christ the *Lord*" (Luke 2:11, emphasis added).

He is both Savior *and* Lord. In fact, it is because he is Lord that he has the authority to be called our Savior.

I know that some people have a real problem with this. They think that Christ's lordship amounts to salvation based on performance, that it goes against the biblical prohibition on judging our neighbor, that it opens the door for individuals and churches to decide for themselves who is truly saved and who is just mouthing the words.

But quite frankly, I don't understand what all the controversy is about. I mean, why would people even *want* to be saved if they didn't want to accept Christ as Lord? In that case, salvation would be nothing more than fire insurance, a self-centered desire to avoid punishment for their sin on *God's* terms while choosing to live the rest of their lives on their *own* terms. Christ made it clear: "No one can be a slave of two masters, since either he will hate one and love the other, or be devoted to one and despise the other" (Matt. 6:24).

We can have but one master. And if that master is not Jesus Christ, yet we insist that we are saved, we are living a lie. Salvation through Christ as the Lord of our lives is the only salvation there is. We simply cannot have one without the other.

ASK ME SOME QUESTIONS

I don't want to get bogged down in this, for most of the ideas and opinions that circulate around this issue do little more than stir up pointless arguments. Then again, I don't want to be misunderstood. Here is where I stand: Christ has done all the hard work of salvation. In no way am I saying—nor does the Bible say—that we must prove our worth or earn our way into God's good graces through our obedience to Christ.

But when God saved you, you really made your last decision, for the moment you came to Jesus Christ as Lord, he assumed the right to direct all your decisions from then on. Your role from that point forward has been to carry them out. He became both your Savior and Lord all at the same time—for all time.

Still, you may have some honest questions, such as:

What about the thief on the cross? He spent his only few minutes or hours as a Christian in the throes of a public execution and never did anything for Christ. Are you saying he wasn't saved? Of course he was saved. Jesus said to him, "I assure you: Today you will be with Me in paradise" (Luke 23:43). Jesus would never have given such false hope to an unsaved person.

I know this: Christ was the Lord of that man's life for whatever brief moments he lived as a believer. In his request of Jesus in verse 42 (though not all Bible translations put it this way), he said: "*Lord,* remember me when You come into Your kingdom" (NKJV, emphasis added). He recognized Jesus as Lord and received him as his Savior. I am also convinced that if some merciful miracle of justice had occurred and the thief had been set free to come down from his cross alive, he would have spent the rest of his days serving his Savior and Lord, who had granted him the ultimate release from his rap sheet of sins.

So can a person put his faith in Jesus with his dying breath and be forgiven of his sins? Absolutely—because no amount of "doing anything" for Christ factors into our salvation. Likewise, the thief's inability to "do anything" for Christ didn't make him any less of a Christian than you or I. He was saved by his faith in Jesus Christ as Savior and Lord—nothing more, but definitely nothing less.

You say we don't have to "do anything" for Christ to become our Savior, but isn't making him our Lord an action on our part? Only in the same sense that *belief* is an action, that *faith* is an action, that *repentance from our sins* is an action. All of these—including our total surrender to Christ as Lord of our lives—are wrapped up in a complete, proper, biblical response to God's love and mercy, which results in our salvation.

I suppose you could label these as "actions" in a very technical sense, but they are better understood as being the small part of the equation we humans bring to the table in this covenant of grace. These responses activate the unstoppable flow of God's cleansing and forgiveness into our hearts and equip us to follow him with pure and holy lives.

You see, in that moment of conversion, he gets it all—every last bit of who we are. That's what salvation is—giving all that we are to all that he is. Nothing is held back. Before we can bat an eye, he instantaneously becomes both our Savior and Lord. That's why when I say (and I'm sure we would both agree) that we can't "do anything" to earn our salvation, I mean that God is not waiting to see a few good deeds start to happen before he stamps our salvation as being official. That would be a misunderstanding of what is meant by Christ's lordship. His lordship constitutes an ongoing relationship with him that changes the way we live. *Christ's lordship is a good thing!* It offers us the freedom to live the full expression of what his salvation has wrought in our hearts.

It's only natural, therefore, that others should be able to see this inner transformation begin to seep into our visible lives. That's what Jesus meant when he referred to a tree being "known by its fruit" (Matt. 12:33). It's what Paul meant when he said that each of us should "examine his own work" (Gal. 6:4). It's what the whole Bible means when God calls on us to deny ourselves; to banish the sin from our lives; to pursue goodness, honesty, and love in all our ways. These things are not *prerequisites* of salvation; they are the *results* of salvation. "For we are His making, created in Christ Jesus for good works, which God prepared ahead of time so that we should walk in them" (Eph. 2:10).

But I don't always do good works. How can I know that I've accepted him as Lord when my life is so far from being perfect? Even though our lives are designed to give evidence of the work of Christ in our hearts, they are not the most reliable evidence of what God has done. "Because if our hearts condemn us, God is greater than our hearts and knows all things" (1 John 3:20).

And our hearts do condemn us. Often. When they do, it should bother the daylights out of us. It should drive us back to our knees in humble anguish, like the Corinthians of whom Paul said, "I am rejoicing, not because you were grieved, but because your grief led to repentance." And look what happened as a result! "For consider how much diligence this very thing—this grieving as God wills—has produced in you: what a desire to clear yourselves, what indignation, what fear, what deep longing, what zeal, what justice! In every way you have commended yourselves to be pure in this matter" (2 Cor. 7:9, 11).

For we would not be invited to "come boldly to the throne of grace" if God never expected us to show up. We would not need a high priest to "sympathize with our weaknesses" if we never had anything we struggled with (Heb. 4:16 NKJV). God already knew when he came to us that he was dealing with wet cement—men and women who find it much easier to be misshapened than to be smoothed and worked into something useful.

However, if you can consistently engage in sinful thoughts and activities as a lifestyle without being upset about it, without sweating over whether you have a problem, without losing a minute's sleep over your failure to live up to your high calling in Christ, then I must tell you as gently as I can that you should seriously examine yourself to see whether you are in the faith (see 2 Cor. 13:5).

On the other hand, if you are angry about the sin in your life, if it grieves your heart the moment you realize what you've done, if the thought of it makes you want to run to the base of that life-giving throne and embrace God's forgiveness with joy, gratitude, and a renewed desire to surrender all to Christ, then you know that God's alarm clock—the Holy Spirit—lives in your heart. You are in there fighting just like the rest of us, fully realizing that you'll never reach perfection until that glorious day "when He appears [and] we will be like Him, because we will see Him as He is." In the meantime "everyone who has this hope in Him purifies himself, just as He is pure" (1 John 3:2–3), knowing that as long as we're here, we can only get better—though not perfect—at letting him live through us.

All of us are works in progress. But thank God, we are at least in progress, being shaped by the ongoing work of Jesus Christ, our Savior and Lord. In this awesome relationship

- he is over us, and we choose to be under;
- he is above us, and we stay beneath;
- he commands, and we give our consent;
- he demands, and we deliver;
- he gives the orders, and we carry them out.

He has given us his all. Therefore, as believers in Christ, we must refuse to limit his lordship or relegate it to an isolated compartment of our lives. We will not only claim to be his with our mouths, but we will live so that his power can be seen in us through our attitudes and actions.

His Lordship Defines
Our Personal Ownership

Does God truly have a right to such total control over us? S. M. Lockridge, a great preacher from the past, once said, "[God] didn't have to put his signature on the corner of the sunrise; he's the owner! He didn't have to put a laundry mark on the lapel of the meadow; he's the owner! He didn't have to carve his initials on the side of a mountain; he's the owner! He didn't have to put his brand on the cattle on a thousand hills; he's the owner! He didn't have to put a copyright on the songs he gave the birds to sing; he is the owner!"

I don't think we fully realize the implications of this. We own nothing—zip! "For we brought nothing into the world, and we can take nothing out" (1 Tim. 6:7). Think of what that means:

- This book you're reading is not yours; it's his. He's given it to you to teach you a little something about who he is and how much he loves you.
- The house you live in is not yours; it's his. He's given it to you to keep you safe and protected and offer you shelter.
- The car you drive is not yours; it's his. He's given it to you to help meet your need for getting from place to place.
- The bed you sleep in is not yours; it's his. He's given it to you to provide a place for you to rest at the end of the day.
- The food in your refrigerator is not yours; it's his. He's given it to you to nourish your body and keep you in good health.

In fact, the refrigerator itself is not yours, the money you paid for it is not yours, the electricity that supplies it with the energy to operate—these are all gifts from your heavenly Father, practical examples of his care and concern about every need in your life.

He owns it all—whether you're a Christian or not. Every breath, every heartbeat, every step, every nerve ending—he made it and he owns it! "The rich and the poor have this in common, the LORD is the maker of them all" (Prov. 22:2).

- He is the Lord of nature. He is the Lord of creation.
- He is the Lord of time. He is the Lord of eternity.
- He is the Lord of life. He is the Lord of death.
- He is the Lord of humanity. He is the Lord of demons.
- He is the Lord of yesterday. He is the Lord of tomorrow.
- He is Lord of all! And he is Lord of you!

As the Jewish man Peter said to the Gentile soldier Cornelius, "The word which God sent to the children of Israel, preaching peace through Jesus Christ—He is *Lord* of all—that word you know" (Acts 10:36–37a NKJV, emphasis added).

As Paul said to the pagan thinkers in Athens, "He has made from one blood every nation of men to dwell on all the face of the earth, and has determined their preappointed times and the boundaries of their dwellings, so that they should seek the *Lord*, in the hope that they might grope for Him and find Him, though He is not far from each one of us; for in Him we live and move and have our being" (Acts 17:26–28a NKJV).

And though we human beings tend to chafe at this invisible authority of God, "ask the beasts, and they will teach you; and the birds of the air, and they will tell you; or speak to the earth, and it will teach you; and the fish of the sea will explain it to you. Who among all these does not know that the hand of the LORD has done this, in whose hand is the life of every living thing, and the breath of all mankind?" (Job 12:7–10).

A LORD BY ANY OTHER NAME

Still, some of us wouldn't be averse to finding a loophole in his lordship. Something seems almost unconstitutional about a government that's not *of* the people, *by* the people, and *for* the people.

But ask yourself this: What happens when we ascribe power to a lord that looks more like us—when we put our own desires in the driver's seat, when we're motivated by acceptance and approval, when we're seduced by the allure of power, pleasure, or greed?

Follow these masters to their inevitable end, and you'll find yourself in a world far different from the one they promised in their promotional brochures. Instead of discovering the evergreen excitement of fun and freedom, you'll find yourself shackled to the long chains of debt and regret. Instead of being content with a new level of income and accessories, you'll find yourself surprisingly unhappy and wanting more. Instead of finding a new batch of friends who won't be so hard to get along with, you'll only succeed in dismantling another set of relationships and leaving yourself even lonelier than you were before.

The devil is a liar. Every phony lord he dangles in front of us leads us right back into the same dismay and disillusionment we were trying to leave—only now we return with even less time to recover, even more apologies to make, and even less of an excuse for being so blind and shortsighted.

There is only one Lord who is "for the people."
How foolish to try replacing him.

THE BEST OF ALL

I try to be careful before saying whether something "always" is or "never" is. Such sweeping generalities are usually undercut by some rare or hypothetical exception that turns my "always" or "never" into a much safer "most of the time." But here I go anyway: I have *never* heard any of those who served the Lord faithfully throughout their lifetime say at the end of their days that they were sorry they had lived for him, that God had failed them, that their efforts as a believer in Christ had all gone to waste. *Never!* (And I never expect to.)

Yet I can think of countless times when I have heard men and women repent for the years they threw away in pursuit of property and portfolios and personal ambition. I've heard them beg the forgiveness of their families and others whom they had hurt, dismissed, or ignored. I've heard them weep over lost opportunities and wish for the chance to correct them.

So you tell me: Which lord do *you* want to follow to the end of your days on earth—one that pretends to have it all but can't deliver it? Or the one who truly owns it all and can deliver you safely into heaven, enabling you to bypass a life of empty pursuits on your way to joy, purpose, and fulfillment?

Jesus Christ is Lord of the people. And better still, he is Lord of all!

HIS LORDSHIP DEMANDS OUR DAILY STEWARDSHIP

Here's where this matter gets extremely, almost painfully, practical. For although we've truly said a mouthful when we declare that Jesus Christ is Lord of our lives, we haven't said much of anything until we've replaced the "our lives" part of that statement with the components that make up our lives. To honestly acknowledge his lordship over us, we must be willing to say things like:

HE IS LORD OF OUR CLOCK

No one has invested more of himself into the hours, minutes, and seconds of our day than Jesus has. He has given his very life to enable us to walk in the freedom of forgiven sin, to prepare us to be a constant example of the changed life he creates in those who believe in him. Beyond that, he has strategically placed us in the locations where we live, work, and play—right down to our street address in the neighborhood, our office arrangement on the city block, our position on the line in the factory, our schedule of classes in the school day, our aerobics session at the health club—all to give us opportunities to shine his light into others' lives.

It's a responsibility we shoulder not only by sharing the gospel through personal evangelism but by doing our work with eagerness and excellence, by reading and relating to our children, by being an available ear to a friend or associate, by looking into the eyes of those we ask "How are you?" and listening long enough to care what their answer is.

The humdrum of routine has a way of stealing the time from our day, subtracting the seconds faster than we can count them. But when we yield our time to the lordship of Christ, he multiplies these fleeting moments into God-ordained seasons of usefulness.

Of course, his lordship also applies to our *free*

time (what little of it there seems to be anymore). This doesn't mean that God wants us laboring around the clock with selfless acts of service, feeling guilty every time we sit down to watch a ball game or go out for ice cream. But it does require a change of perspective on the way we spend our spare moments, asking God to show us what he wants us doing with each part of our day, then trusting that he will answer us in ways that unexpectedly meet the needs of others while fully accommodating our own need for rest and refreshment.

HE IS ALSO LORD OF OUR CALENDAR

We're quick to talk about what we're going to do this summer, where we're going to go for the holidays, or how we're going to get away this weekend. We shape our expectations of life around certain priorities, then we fill in our datebooks to match them.

But Christ, being the Lord of our lives, is also Lord of our priorities. And because he is Lord of our priorities, he is also the Lord of our plans. As Christians, we simply cannot set our goals about where we are going to be in five years—or even make tight arrangements about where we're going to be this Friday—without seeking to know the will of our Lord and King.

But again, while this can seem foreign to our ordinary way of thinking, restrictive to our freedom to go and to do, nothing is more liberating than letting Christ be the Lord of our schedules. Only he possesses the wisdom to see all things perfectly, and only he knows what is truly best for us. We may think we know what we need to be doing, but only God knows its full ramifications. When we allow him to set our priorities and plan our itineraries, he can take us to places of growth and opportunity we never knew existed.

HE IS ALSO LORD OF OUR CHECKBOOK

I know this hurts a little bit. We usually save this subject for last, not wanting to get around to it until we have to. But our feet really shouldn't get so cold about this because God has a purpose for the money he has given us. It is a plan that promises blessing to both us and our fellowman. And no self-centered scheme of our own can possibly be better for us in the long run than the heavenly ideals God has shown us in his Word concerning our money. If we will get these truths into our hearts—if we will believe and practice them—we will enter an area of victory that many of us have never found before in our Christian lives.

1. *We own nothing; God owns everything.* "For the world is Mine," God says, "and all its fullness" (Ps. 50:12). Everything we have, God has given us. Someone else's name may be signed on our paycheck, but God alone has endorsed it over to him.

2. *Although we are an owner of nothing, we are a steward of everything.* Here is God's command: "Based on the gift they have received, everyone should use it to serve others, as good managers of the varied grace of God" (1 Pet. 4:10). The dollars are his; they're not ours to automatically turn into football tickets or a new outfit. They're not ours to claim for any careless purpose we desire. We have been entrusted a measure of heavenly bounty, and we must be careful to use it for heavenly good.

3. *We will only have in heaven what we have given to God on earth.* You see, the lordship of Christ forms the foundation for everything we do in this life. And

34

according to the Scripture, what we build on that foundation has a direct bearing on our future reward (see 1 Cor. 3:9–15). Some of that building will be constructed of "gold, silver, and precious stones"—the things we invested in the kingdom of God, the money we sacrificed so that others could have enough, the resources we used in order to prepare our children for Christian service. But the Bible calls *some* of our building materials "wood, hay, and straw"—the stuff we basically spent on ourselves, the DVD system we bought for our den, the new drapes to match the new carpet in the living room. God is not saying that we can never enjoy these things; he's just reminding us that they have no eternal value—that the next time we get a little extra money in, treating ourselves shouldn't always or necessarily be our first response.

Christ has become the Lord of our lives, both spiritually speaking *and* practically speaking. He is Lord of all, and that means *all* that we have.

HIS LORDSHIP DECIDES
OUR ETERNAL FELLOWSHIP

Get this picture.

We're all in God's throne room—millions and billions of people—yet the air is hushed and still, the frailty of humanity in stunned awe of the Almighty. Suddenly the silence is broken by the swift, rippling sound of wings folding. It's the angels bending their knees. And if you listen hard enough, you even notice that the demons in hell have ceased their cackling, their legs beginning to weaken and tremble, their own knees falling to meet the sulfurous cinders of hell's bottom floor.

The moment is electric. Your lips can hardly contain the rush of worship welling up inside you. The one with "the name that is above every name" (Phil. 2:9) has taken his place at the right hand of the Father, and the chorus of the ages has begun lifting their song—their final, four-word song—"Jesus Christ is Lord!"

"Jesus Christ is Lord!"

Some are spitting it through clenched teeth—Judas, Mohammed, Hitler, Napoleon. What many had refused to believe on earth, they are shouting at the top of their lungs in eternity.

But we who surrendered our all to him, we who praised him as our Savior and submitted to him as Lord, cannot stop long enough to stare at the spectacle. We are too enraptured ourselves, too lost in repeating those same four words through tears of utter joy, "Jesus Christ is Lord!"

"Jesus Christ is Lord!"

Would we have dared miss this? Would we have demanded our freedom from Christ's lordship only to find ourselves declaring it when we could only regret it? Would we have run from Christ's authority, not realizing it was our only source of protection?

Make me a captive, Lord,
And then I shall be free;
Force me to render up my sword,
And I shall conqueror be.

OUR SACRED HONOR

The sword was historically considered to be the most personal weapon an officer could carry. To surrender one's sword, therefore, was a token of complete surrender. In fact, if an officer was discovered to have disgraced the force, his commander was obligated to take away the man's sword—snapping the blade in two as a token of the officer's break from the military ranks.

British admiral Lord Nelson, after a notable victory over the French, demanded that the French admiral appear before him to surrender. The vanquished foe had no choice but to agree. Yet at the place of their arranged meeting, the enemy soldier strode proudly across the deck of a British ship, a smirk on his face, his sword dangling from his side. Stiffly, he thrust his beefy hand toward the stoic figure of Lord Nelson, offering a conciliatory handshake as a casual act of friendship. But Lord Nelson remained unmoved, his hands hanging calmly at his side as he spoke these words victoriously to the defeated Frenchman: "First, your sword, sir."

Is your sword still hanging from *your* belt—the sword you're using to fight your way through life, the sword you're using to battle Christ for first place in your affections, the sword you're using to establish the ground around you as off-limits to Christ's lordship?

The Lord Jesus is asking for your sword. He's asking for the thing you hold closest to your vest—your clock, your calendar, your checkbook, whatever. He's asking for the keys to your heart, the throne of your life. For when he is on that throne, you are truly in his hand.

And you can't get any safer than that.

CHAPTER 3

THE KING AND HIS KINGDOM

Living a Kingdom-Minded Life

One of the main starting points in living under the lord-ship of Christ is understanding what matters most to him. We're not totally unfamiliar with this kind of exercise.

- When we begin to work for someone, we quickly find out what our new boss considers important.
- When we're trying to interest a client in the item or service we provide, the first phase of our homework is to discover what his main objectives are.
- When a performer is being trained by a special-ized teacher, the lessons will do nothing but grind the student into frustration until she learns what the teacher is really looking for.

So . . . what would you say is of chief importance to Christ?

We don't have to look far into his life to find out.

WHAT MATTERS MOST TO CHRIST

Step into the Gospel of Matthew, the very first pages of the New Testament. Climb over the long list of begats; take a Christmas journey with Mary, Joseph, and the wise men; see Jesus come to the Jordan to be baptized; hear him battle Satan's grueling temptations in the wilderness, then watch him emerge with his very first words to a waiting world: "Repent, because the kingdom of heaven has come near" (Matt. 4:17). And if he said it once, he said it a thousand times.

Over and over and over again, Jesus returned to this theme throughout his earthly ministry. This man whom Herod once sought as being "King of the Jews" would prove to be King over much more—he would be revealed as King over a spiritual kingdom that knows no end and a King who tolerates no rivals.

But what is this kingdom, and why is it so important to Christ?

Is It Magic?

Perhaps the most famous kingdom on our planet today is Walt Disney World's Magic Kingdom. It's a place where everything is clean, everyone is nice, and all news is happy news. The only work is play and the sole object is fun.

It's a nice place to visit.

But no one can really live there. Because it's a make-believe kingdom, a pretend paradise, the nostalgic dream day always comes to a close, usually with a traffic jam in the parking lot. The only thing that's really magic is how fast our money disappears at the ticket booth and the concession stand.

The kingdom of God, however, doesn't depend on magic; it is totally dependent on its Master. Christ Jesus is its King and Lord. He rules and reigns over it as completely and confidently today as he has from eternity past.

- It's a kingdom of lasting peace and joy, not war and sadness.
  - It's a kingdom of authentic wholeness and love, not sickness and hatred.
  - It's a kingdom of eternal life and faith, not fear and death.

We don't always see it in this form, of course, because the kingdom of God is largely invisible to the human eye. It is often hidden in mystery, incapable of being measured within an average lifetime. Its truths reside in a mine much deeper than man's wisdom and philosophy, confounding those who seek to understand it as they would a mathematics equation or a science experiment.

For how (some would say) can anyone with a critical thought in his head concede the existence of a place where the lion lays down with the lamb, where the child can pick up a snake as a plaything, where the wolf stops feeding *on* the sheep and chooses instead to feed *alongside* the sheep?

I know it makes no sense. It causes the cynical mind to rub its eyes, shake its head, and look twice before it can believe what it's seeing. But these are the kinds of things that happen with regularity in the kingdom of God—when Christ is allowed to rule in the life of a person or a church.

The Impossible Becomes Possible

The call goes out, as it did from Jesus to his first followers: "As you go, announce this: 'The kingdom of heaven has come near.' Heal the sick, raise the dead, cleanse the lepers, cast out demons" (Matt. 10:7–8). And amazingly (not by magic but by the sheer authority of God's Word), the miracle of Christian unity and hope begins to change the definition of *impossible:* lives are restored and homes are regained—and all because the rule of Christ has again taken effect, with astounding results.

This is what pleases Jesus.

So where people are surrendered to his kingship, he graces us by peeling back the curtain a little on his kingdom, letting us see it here and there, in bits and snatches—the power of God counteracting the trial and error of ordinary living.

And if you have received Christ as Savior and Lord, you are a citizen of that kingdom. Jesus is your King, and you have certain responsibilities to fulfill. But you can be assured that everything you invest in the work of God's kingdom will reap rewards that stretch far into eternity.

RELATING TO GOD'S KINGDOM

The kingdom of God is at the very heart of what Christ wants to do through you. But the question remains—just how do we, his visible subjects, relate to this invisible kingdom?

WE MUST SEE THE REALITY OF THE KINGDOM

Ask most people to define the kingdom of God, and the answer will probably come back a little cloudy. Talk about it over the lunch table, and while some may nod their heads and agree with you in theory, they'll likely be hard pressed to see the kingdom as a concrete reality.

But there obviously must be an actual kingdom. Surely Jesus wasn't just filling our heads with wishful thinking when he told us to "seek first the kingdom of God" (Matt. 6:33). In fact, this very phrase—"kingdom of God" or "kingdom of heaven"—shows up more than sixty times in the Gospels, eighty-five times altogether in the New Testament. Proclaiming its presence was Christ's stated reason for being here: "I must proclaim the good news about the kingdom of God . . . because I was sent for this purpose" (Luke 4:43).

And that's not all he said about it:

- We already know it formed the main subject for some of his first recorded words in Scripture.
- He taught us to pray regularly to the Father, asking that "Your kingdom come" (Matt. 6:10).
- He declared that the persecuted and the poor in spirit were partakers in it "because theirs is the kingdom of heaven" (see Matt. 5).
- He told dozens of parables about it, using the well-worn figures of sowers, sheep, and mustard seeds to explain the kingdom so people could understand it.
- And guess what he was talking about during the last few days before his ascension? He was "speaking about the kingdom of God" (Acts 1:3)—a kingdom that is given to us by the "Father's good pleasure" (Luke 12:32 NKJV).

I could go on and on because this one line of thinking clearly dominated the teachings and sayings of Christ. It was his passion, his message, his vision. He went out of his way to make clear to us that the kingdom of God is real and its rule is revolutionary.

But even if you can accept that the kingdom of God is real, you may wonder:

- Is it something we can truly experience today?
- Or is it a realm of existence we won't enter until some point in the future?

The Bible's simplest answer to both of these questions is: Yes.

It is a coming kingdom. At the Last Supper, Jesus said to his disciples, "I will no longer drink of the fruit of the vine until that day when I drink it new in the kingdom of God" (Mark 14:25). That statement certainly has a future ring about it. Joseph of Arimathea, the Jewish council member who asked for Jesus' body in order to give it a proper burial, was described in the Gospels as being "a good and righteous man . . . who was looking forward to the kingdom of God" (Luke 23:50–51). There is a fullness to God's kingdom that can never be known as long as we're here on earth.

But the kingdom eludes easy definition. For while it is certainly a final reign of God that is still to come, it is also a present reality in the lives of his people. Were it only a future existence, how could Jesus have said of himself—even before his death and resurrection—"If I drive out demons by the finger of God, then the kingdom of God has come to you" (Luke 11:20). Or "being asked by the Pharisees when the kingdom of God will come, He answered them, 'The kingdom of God is not coming with something observable; no one will say, "Look here!" or "There!" For you see, the kingdom of God is among you'" (Luke 17:20–21).

We who are bought with the blood of Christ are already tasting the firstfruits of his kingdom, yet we can accurately say in the same breath that his kingdom is still to come, and "His kingdom will have no end" (Luke 1:33).

IS THE CHURCH THE KINGDOM?

Some have said that the present incarnation of God's kingdom is the church. While it's true that the church is called by God to concern itself with kingdom business, the two are not the same.

The church is not to preach the church; it is to preach the gospel of the kingdom. As Jesus proclaimed, "This good news of the kingdom will be proclaimed in all the world as a testimony to all nations" (Matt. 24:14). The gospel that the church is commanded to preach is the gospel of the kingdom—an eternal reality that is *present* in God's people but is not the *same thing* as God's people.

Think of it like this. When you hold an apple in your hand, you are not holding the apple tree. You're merely seeing its fruit—the result of natural reproduction that places into the apple all the identifying marks of the tree. The fruit bears the tree's flavor and nutrients; it extends the tree's influence to other parts of the world; it even speaks of the wonders of the tree's Creator. But the apple is merely a messenger, a product of its source. It can serve a lot of satisfactory purposes, but it cannot be the tree.

In the same way the church is Christ's agent in the world. It is grounded in Christ—fully dependent on Christ—and it performs the work of his kingdom. It can do many glorious things within this remarkable relationship, but it *cannot be the kingdom*. The kingdom is much bigger and broader than the church itself.

What does all of this mean to you and me? Our first goal in life as believers is to be *Christ-centered*. As long as we remain focused on him, believing on him, seeking to honor and obey him with our lives, he will lead us toward becoming people who are *kingdom-minded* in all of our ways. Why?—because as we have seen, the kingdom is of primary importance to Christ, and he will never lead us to do anything that is not best for his kingdom.

Yet as we become more kingdom-minded, we should find ourselves also becoming more *church-based*, working together with our brothers and sisters in Christ to extend the kingdom's influence in our cities, towns, and communities. (We'll talk in much more detail about this in the next chapter.) Our primary motivation for doing this, however, is not to promote the church. We work through the church—God's army on the ground in the world—because, and *only* because, we have first caught a glimpse of the kingdom, and we are hungry to see that kingdom come and increase. Yes, the church is the seat of Christ's authority in the earth. Its mission, however, is to tell others *not* about itself but about its King and about his kingdom.

WE MUST SEEK THE RULE OF THE KINGDOM

The word *kingdom* literally refers to the rule and reign of a king. We tend to think of kingdom in terms of territory or land area—the actual real estate governed by the king of a country. But even in this sense, the king's rule is not so much over acreage as it is over people. He has authority over his subjects, and through them he controls all that they have.

Similarly, yet in a much deeper sense, we are Christ's subjects in his kingdom.

How do you feel about that word? *Subjects.*

In many ways, a son obeys his father because he *wants* to. A servant obeys his master because he *needs* to. But a subject obeys his king because he *has* to. He has no other choice. The king's control is complete; his will is both sovereign and supreme. His wish is our command.

Apparently, though, the subjects do maintain an option of sorts. We know of a time in Jesus' life when "many of His disciples turned back and no longer walked with Him." Seeing these followers pulling back from him, "Jesus said to the Twelve, 'You don't want to go away too, do you?' Simon Peter answered, 'Lord, to whom should we go? You have the words of eternal life. And we have come to believe and know that You are the Holy One of God!'" (John 6:66–68).

So we do have an option, I guess. Even if we couldn't read it in the Bible, we already know it from experience. We know of times in our own lives when we have drawn back from Christ, unwilling to pay the price of discipleship, deceived into thinking we could find another master who wouldn't demand so much of us. But, as Peter said, "To whom should we go?" What other option is open to us if we hope to live at peace? The happiest subjects of the kingdom are not those who have flung Christ's authority from their shoulders but those who have surrendered their lives to his control.

Our option as believers then is not to choose whether we will be Christ's subjects. Our option is to choose whether we will be happy or miserable ones.

His Rightful Throne. Our hearts are a throne, a seat made for a king, a throne that cannot go unoccupied. Someone is always going to be sitting in that lofty position of authority, administering rule over our lives. Too often, however, the face we see on that throne is the same one we see when we brush our teeth in the morning. It *looks* like us because it *is* us.

And I'm here to tell you, we make lousy kings.

Until we are willing to take our stubborn hands off the reins of our lives and abdicate the throne to one who has earned that place by right and reputation, we will continue to live like those desperate souls unfortunate enough to reside in nations led by fools and tyrants.

You've seen them on the news. Their citizens are in the streets, either begging for relief or being bullied by agents of their hostile regimes. Their children starve for lack of food and nourishment. Their livelihood being too meager to lift them out of poverty, basic needs go unmet day after sorrowful day, year after unending year. And perhaps the most terrifying parts are the stories not revealed by broadcast cameras: the unseen, unheard accounts of imprisonment and torture, shameful acts of power inflicted on the weak and helpless.

We are just like these tyrannized citizens, my friend, when we let ourselves rule from the throne of our hearts. Our inner man, though not always loud enough to be heard, begins to starve and waste away. Our children lose the living, breathing witness of Christian testimony in the home and are forced to make do on the empty husks of religious ritual. Over time—even if no one else sees it—the darkness begins to surround us, life

47

throws us a curve we don't know how to handle, and we sink into despair with nothing to stop our fall.

It is at points like these when we call out to God, "Lord, help me. I'm making such a huge mess of this. I need you to come and take control of my life. *Your kingdom come!"*

Yet in order for us to truly say, "Your kingdom come," we must be willing to complete the sentence by also saying this: "My kingdom goes."

If he is to rule, we must relent.

Joy in the Kingdom. Years ago when I was visiting in London, England, I had the opportunity to see Buckingham Palace. The moment I arrived, I instinctively looked for the flagpole to see whether the queen was in residence.

Like you, perhaps, I was remembering this from my history books: Back in the days of lords and ladies, of kingdoms and castles, of knights in shining armor, there was an understood custom that enabled the people in the street to know when the king had returned from the hunt or the battlefield. Whenever he was physically in his palace, actually seated on the throne of power, the colors of the king—the royal flag—would be seen flying from the top of the castle.

In much the same way, a flag flaps in the wind over *our* lives when Christ the King is at home in our hearts. When he isn't there, the flagpole stands empty; the testimony of our Christian life and witness appears bland and pointless, almost invisible. But when Jesus is actively at work in us—ruling, directing, and orchestrating—the color begins to return to our cheeks, the substance begins to show in our words and responses, and the flag of joy begins to snap in the breeze of God's holiness.

Yes, *joy* is the flag that flies from the castle of our hearts when Christ is in residence. No other king can cause this to occur. Only Jesus can make his subjects lift their heads from their work, look above to their Master, and sing—for joy.

Seek and You Shall Find. This is great because it means we don't have to aggressively go out seeking joy in order to find it. Joy just comes along as a by-product when we seek God's kingdom.

Most people spend the better part of the day seeking their own personal good, yet they come home at night with little to show for it. When seeking the kingdom is our number-one goal, however, joy simply shows up at the back door.

Christ's kingdom should come before everything. Remember how Jesus put it? "Seek *first* the kingdom of God" (Matt. 6:33, emphasis added). This *seeking* is a present tense verb that means "to actively pursue, to go after." And you can be sure, when Jesus tells us to "go after" something, he intends for us to do it with all our might—at the expense of everything else. Jesus is not interested in being some kind of runner-up or second-in-command in our lives. He is our King—and his kingdom gets it all.

But you may ask, "What does *seeking the kingdom* look like? How do I do that in practical terms?"

•   First, seek the glory of the King. Worship him. I don't mean just singing songs to him at church. The Bible says, "Whether you eat or drink, or whatever you do, do everything for God's glory" (1 Cor. 10:31). We worship him simply by doing our jobs well, by taking care of our bodies, by making time for our families— time that might otherwise go to ourselves and our own interests. When we begin every task of an ordinary day by deliberately committing it to God's glory, asking that he be honored by our efforts and be clearly seen in what we do, we are actively seeking the kingdom.

I know it sounds almost too easy! *You mean, I'm seeking the kingdom just by doing for him what I do every day?* Yes, that's exactly what I'm saying! Seeking the kingdom isn't reserved for super Christians who do super things. The kingdom is sought and found every hour, every moment, by everyday people who turn a wrench, take an order, or teach a class. You can seek his glory in the next five minutes, while you're reading this book, by doing even *this* simple task for the glory of God.

• Second, seek the guidance of the King. Obviously, this requires thinking about life in a much different manner than most people do. That's why the Bible advises us not to "be conformed to this age, but be transformed by the renewing of your mind, that you may discern what is the good, pleasing, and perfect will of God" (Rom. 12:2). As loyal subjects of the King, we should want nothing more than to know God's perfect will, to know exactly what he wants us to do, and then to do it. So "if any of you lacks wisdom, he should ask God, who gives to all generously and without criticizing" (James 1:5).

This doesn't mean God always shows us what to do immediately. He knows (better than we) what we need and when we need it. But even in the act of seeking his guidance, we are seeking his kingdom. We are looking beyond ourselves, looking past our own hunches and guesses, looking for the wisdom of God that can turn one of our problems or questions into an opening for his glory. The very act of prayer—real, Christ-centered prayer—is one of the most effective and practical ways to seek God's kingdom.

• Finally, seek the government of the King. Let him have control of what you do. Open your calendar in the morning and ask him to take charge of the day before you. Pause before your next appointment and entrust every second of the time to his care. When you say the blessing at the dinner table, ask God to do whatever he wants with the time you're spending together as a family tonight.

This is not slavery to a micromanaging Master. This is opening your arms wide to the loving leadership of your Lord and King, becoming an active participant in his plans for your corner of the world, shaking yourself loose from the chokehold of sin so that you can experience the liberty of life in his kingdom.

You will find his rule to be one of the greatest rewards of your salvation.

WE MUST SHOW THE RIGHTEOUSNESS OF THE KINGDOM

We have clearly seen that one of our main responsibilities in the kingdom requires that we submit to the rule of the King, surrendering ourselves to the lordship of Christ. But for this to actually happen, we must be true to the second phrase of Christ's command: to "seek first the kingdom of God *and* His righteousness" (Matt. 6:33, emphasis added).

You see, our task is not merely to desire God's control over us but to display his character within us. The kingdom is not just to be inwardly enjoyed and experienced but to be outwardly expressed. "Even a child," the Bible says, "is known by his deeds, whether what he does is pure and right" (Prov. 20:11).

This turns out to be one of the best ways for us to know whether we are seeking the kingdom. Is Christ's righteousness coming out in the daily comings and goings of our day? Are our actions yielding the proof of a changed, transformed heart? Are we "taking every thought captive to the obedience of Christ"? (2 Cor. 10:5).

A Healthy Fear of God. Some years ago the editors of a leading London newspaper became angry at the disturbing number of typographical errors that were going out uncorrected in their daily editions. They took several stabs at addressing the problem, but nothing worked. The papers continued to filter into the city each day, marred by mistakes.

Then the editors got an idea. They told the typesetters that under a new policy, the first copy of each day's paper would be delivered personally to the king. He would be reading it the first thing every morning.

Can you guess what happened next? The paper became virtually error free. Why? Because the workers began laboring under a new set of expectations. They suddenly had a renewed sense of personal responsibility, realizing that the words they placed on the page would be coming under the direct scrutiny of the king. They knew that a halfway job was not going to be good enough.

Whether we realize it or not, we live each day under the scrutiny of our King. His eye is upon us to build into us the expectation that we have a holy Lord to follow. A halfway job is just not going to cut it. We will shortchange our reason for being here by failing to live up to the standards of his righteousness.

Doing Good. But notice that it is "His" righteousness we are to seek, not ours.

It's a sad, highly unpopular truth of life that "there is no one righteous, not even one; there is no one who understands; there is no one who seeks God. All have turned away. Together they have become useless; there is no one who does good, there is not even one" (Rom. 3:10–12).

Pity, because many people in this world are banking their futures on these verses being false.

Yet these words are very, very true. And were it not for God doing something to solve this problem, these words would leave us no hope of obeying the "seeking his righteousness" clause in our Christian contract. There's good news, however: Because we have received Christ Jesus as Savior and Lord, we have been given the freedom—(yes, that's the word that best describes it)— the *freedom* to show forth his righteousness. His high expectation of us is not a dead weight around our neck but a rush of fresh air in our sails. It is our only chance of turning this life of ours into something profitable.

We have no righteousness to offer. How frustrating it would be, then, if God had commanded us to do good, but try as we might, we had nothing good to bring before him. We could never satisfy our responsibilities in the kingdom.

But that's not what God is demanding. He isn't asking us to work up a resumé of good deeds. He's just asking us to sweep out the remaining holdovers of sin in our lives so that *his* goodness has a nice, clean place to operate, so that he can transform these hands, arms, and feet into living instruments of his righteousness.

We have not been called to *perform* for our King but to be *transformed* into conduits of his purity and holiness. We who are seeking his kingdom are also seeking his righteousness—and becoming more amazed by the day at what our King can accomplish as he works through us.

WE MUST SHARE THE RULER OF THE KINGDOM

What a blessing to be a citizen of this kingdom!

What an honor and privilege it is to be a child of God!

What a joy to be able to live with the risen Lord at work in us!

How can we keep from wanting to pass this on? We who have been invited to *enter* the kingdom should be equally as animated and eager about *extending* the kingdom—doing all we can to show others how wonderful it is to have Christ on the throne of our hearts.

This is what matters to Jesus.

This is what should matter to us.

- More than we want to extend the life of our cars and appliances, we should want to extend the life of our Savior and Lord to our friends, family, and neighbors.

- More than we want to extend the reach of our business, we should want to extend the reach of

God's kingdom into our circles and areas of influence.

- More than we want to extend our buying power into our retirement years, we should want our money to extend beyond our own death, investing it in those who are carrying this life-saving gospel to the nations . . . and from them to the next person . . . and from them to the next.

We have not been received into Christ's kingdom merely to enjoy its fringe benefits and to relax in its rewards, but to seek others with whom we can share its wealth.

Time Marches On. Many modern-day Christians shy away from mentioning this for fear of sounding too alarmist, too hard-line. But one of the most compelling reasons for getting busy about sharing Christ is that we don't have forever to do it. The Ruler of this kingdom is coming again: "Then comes the end, when He hands over the kingdom to God the Father, when He abolishes all rule and all authority and power" (1 Cor. 15:24).

I want you to stop for a second and realize that this is actually going to happen. "For the Lord Himself will descend from heaven with a shout, with the archangel's voice, and with the trumpet of God, and the dead in Christ will rise first" (1 Thess. 4:16). I don't know when it's going to happen. No one but the Father does. But one day all the things we have grown accustomed to on earth will "pass away with a loud noise, the elements will burn and be dissolved, and the earth and the works on it will be disclosed" (2 Pet. 3:10).

Many people live as though this event will never occur. Yet were they to think of it—being resistant to the grace of God and therefore outside his saving mercies—the prospect of such a final calamity could cause them nothing but abject fear and horror. Like the ten virgins in Jesus' parable, they are not ready for the bridegroom to come, and when the door shuts, they'll have no way and no words to cause it to open again.

Put faces on these people. Perhaps they're your relatives, your parents, your children. Perhaps they work in the cubicle next to yours or shop in the same supermarket. Perhaps they sit near you at the ball game or change the oil in your automobile or walk your block every evening. If they are without Christ, they are without hope, without a chance . . . .

But not without warning—for they have you in their lives. They have the visible witness of someone who knows what life in this kingdom is like, who knows the way that can lead them to salvation, who knows the King personally and is eager to introduce them to him. They have a person in their life who can look at the certain end of our earthly existence and anticipate it with joy, knowing that it marks the momentous occasion when "the kingdoms of this world . . . become the kingdoms of our Lord and of His Christ, and He shall reign forever and ever" (Rev. 11:15 NKJV). "And He will wipe away every tear from their eyes. Death will exist no longer; grief, crying, and pain will exist no longer, because the previous things have passed away" (Rev. 21:4).

They have you—and they need your King. Today more than yesterday. Now more than ever. The Spirit alone will do the calling, but we must be ready for him to do his calling through us.

THY KINGDOM COME

Thomas More wrote a book in 1516 entitled *Utopia*. In that book he described an imaginary ideal society that was free from poverty, suffering, pain, and sorrow. It's interesting to me that the word *utopia* comes from a Greek word that literally means "no place"—which is quite frankly the only place on earth we'll ever achieve it.

That's because a utopia is a dream. It's the best that any mortal who cares about his fellowman can conceive, but it can never be anything more than a sheer impossibility. True, we should support those who are laboring for the peace of the world, those who are meeting the physical needs of the sick and the dying. We should be involved in efforts that feed, clothe, and shelter the destitute of our planet.

But they need no food more desperately than the bread of the gospel. They need no news more inviting than the good news of Jesus Christ. He is their only hope for a better life, for a place where all can come to be fed and cared for, where all are welcome—in his kingdom.

Can you imagine a place where Jesus rules as King and Lord over everyone—a place where every last human being is fully surrendered to the control of Christ? That place would be heaven. We're going there someday. And we must do all we can to take a bunch of people with us.

"Since all these things are to be destroyed in this way, it is clear what sort of people you should be in holy conduct and godliness" (2 Pet. 3:11). We should be people who are seeking the king, submitting to his rule, showing forth his righteousness . . . .

And saying his message loud enough so that everyone can hear.

This is life in the kingdom. And this is what pleases Jesus.

CHAPTER 4

THE KING
AND HIS CASTLE

Living a Church-Based Life

There were seven of them. The wonders of the ancient world.

- The Hanging Gardens of Babylon—lush terraces of greenery and tree groves, artificially transplanted into the flat, arid regions of modern Iraq
- The Statue of Zeus at Olympia—sixty feet of gleaming ivory, towering above his worshipers on a jewel-studded throne.
- The Temple of Artemis at Ephesus—for centuries a place of pilgrimage for the people of Asia Minor, its magnificence enclosing a palatial site the size of a football field
- The Mauseleum at Halicarnassus—the spectacular tomb of King Maussollos, topped by a stunning statue of the king and his wife in a horse-drawn chariot
- The Colossus of Rhodes—one hundred feet of hollow bronze honoring the sun god Helios, guarding the city's harbor and visible for miles out at sea

- The Pharos of Alexandria—a four-hundred-foot white stone tower lighthouse on Egypt's Mediterranean coast, a fire constantly ablaze from its uppermost story
- The Pyramids of Giza—a series of enormous limestone tombs rising from the sands of Egypt, the only one of these great landmarks that still remains

Earthquake, fire, and the advancing armies of foreign invaders toppled all but one of these world-renowned structures, leaving behind little more than their likenesses as etchings on old coins. One of the ancient wonders even collapsed into shards of metal to be sold off the scrap heap. These grandiose works were legendary, but they were not lasting.

There are other wonders, too, that have been recognized as being civilization's finest work, such as the Colosseum of Rome, the Parthenon of Greece, and Petra (the City of Rock) in Jordan. These wonders have been in many ways eclipsed by such modern wonders as Big Ben, the Eiffel Tower, the Empire State Building, the Golden Gate Bridge, the Statue of Liberty, the Suez Canal, and others. Time and tourism have also given "wonder" status to such natural works of art as the Grand Canyon and Niagara Falls.

I have been blessed with the opportunity to see each of these present-day wonders. The immense skill, artistry, and labor of those who created them are truly amazing. And of course, the beauty and grandeur of God's natural wonders are stunning, breathtaking.

But stand any of these wonders next to the church

of the living God—or stand all of them end-to-end—
and they pale in comparison.

WHAT'S SO WONDERFUL
ABOUT THE CHURCH?

You may think that's crazy. Perhaps the church has
become for you a boring matter of routine. The sermons, the classes, the same old thing. Oh, every once in
awhile—at Easter, maybe, when there's music and
drama and pageantry—maybe then it has that "wonderful" look and feel about it. But the church on an every-
day/every-week basis . . . a wonder?

Perhaps, in fact, it's been your experience that the
closer you got to the inner workings of the church, the
more you came away not impressed and inspired but
disappointed and disillusioned. The world's wonders
have precision and grace, but the church seems to be
characterized more by disharmony and disagreement,
by hypocrisy, petty wranglings, and hallway gossip. You
like the church, you're *committed* to the church, but
being a *part* of the church sometimes takes a lot more
effort than it seems it should.

I understand that.

But I want you to try pulling away for a moment,
looking past the people and personalities, thinking bigger than what you see with your eyes or remember
from your childhood, and begin seeing the church for
what it really is—and whose it really is.

I want you to catch the wonder again. I want to
exhort you to see the church of God in the same way
the God of the church sees it.

LET US EXALT
THE FOUNDER OF THE CHURCH

You've probably heard it said, "The church is not a building; the church is its people." And that's very true. But I believe the first place to look to see the wonder of the church is not toward its people (as sweet, kind, and thoughtful as they may be—or as harsh, stern, and bull-headed as they may be) but toward its Founder and Leader, its reason for being.

The church—your church—belongs to Jesus Christ. And it is from him that the church derives its wonder because

- he is its strength, its source, and its Savior;
- he is the life and truth that both supports and sustains it;
- he has assumed the responsibility for carrying it safely into the future;
- and he has secured its victory for all eternity.

You see, I could tell you in all honesty that the church is the largest institution that has ever existed on the face of the earth. Current research indicates that nearly 1.9 billion people in the world today profess faith in the Lord Jesus Christ. I could take a giant step further and tell you that by the end of the twenty-first century—at the present rate of growth—approximately *five* billion people will be members of the visible church on the earth. And these numbers don't take into account the untold millions of others who have already died in Christ and are dwelling even now in his very presence. These are staggering numbers—surprising to some—and in one sense they go a long way toward impressing the unconvinced that the church is not on the way out but, rather, on the way up.

However, we who are members of the church don't have to rely on our numbers to give us weight and significance. We don't have to depend on acceptance and popularity in order to consider ourselves part of something valuable and important.

We must merely see Jesus. He is all the glory the church ever needs.

Look carefully into his eyes again and hear what he has to say about his church.

CHRIST AND THE CHURCH

Remember the time Jesus sat down with his disciples and asked them this question?

> "Who do men say that I, the Son of Man, am?"
>
> So they said, "Some say John the Baptist, some Elijah, and others Jeremiah or one of the prophets."
>
> He said to them, "But who do you say that I am?"
>
> Simon Peter answered and said, "You are the Christ, the Son of the living God."
>
> Jesus answered and said to him, "Blessed are you, Simon Bar-Jonah, for flesh and blood has not revealed this to you, but My Father who is in heaven. And I also say to you that you are Peter, and on this rock I will build My church, and the gates of Hades shall not prevail against it." (Matt. 16:13–18 NKJV)

This short scene from the life of Christ yields some profound insights into his view of the church—both the things that are of importance to him and the things that don't interest him at all.

First, Christ is not concerned about public opinion. The initial question he put to his disciples was not intended as a way to gather poll results. For one thing, he was already fully aware of what people were saying about him. Even more than the words they were saying, he understood the heart and motive behind those who were slandering his existence and mocking his ministry. More than likely, Jesus was just wanting to see the look in his followers' eyes as they reported what they were hearing—the look that probably betrayed some of their own feelings about this so-called Son of God who was sitting before them.

Were they not so sure themselves? Were they inwardly wondering whether there might be some truth in what the people on the street were saying? Perhaps he *was* merely a sideshow attraction, not the one who was "appointed heir of all things . . . the radiance of [God's] glory, the exact expression of His nature . . . sustain[ing] all things by His powerful word" (Heb. 1:2–3).

We don't know all the reasons Jesus had for asking this question, but we know he wasn't trying to win the respect of the press or hoping to draw a bigger crowd at his next public event. The opinions of others were immaterial to the one-goal focus that drove him to remain obedient to his Father—up to, through, and beyond the very end.

And he is no more concerned about public opinion today.

Count on the newspapers to pigeonhole the church into an out-of-date, old-school, uninspiring shell of religious expression that has no influence or relevance in a modern age.

Never be surprised to see the TV documentaries jump at the chance to deride, berate, and expose the church's failings and weaknesses, painting us all with the same broad brush as those who indeed bring disgrace on the cause of Christ.

Don't get discouraged when the bulk of the people on your street are either sleeping, eating breakfast, or mowing the grass when you drive by their houses on Sunday morning. Right now, they may see the church as a pointless interruption in an otherwise relaxing weekend. They may not understand what anybody gets out of it. We'll continue to pray for them, stop by to visit them, and share the gospel of the kingdom with them every chance we get. But if some of them never have a brighter view of God's people than they do today, it will not diminish the power of the church or slow its march toward a victorious eternity. The church's authority does not rest on the whim of majority rule but on the authority of its Lord and Ruler.

Nevertheless, Christ is concerned with our personal conviction. The key question in this conversation between Jesus and his followers is the second one—not "Who do *men* say that I am?" but "Who do *you* say that I am?" He wasn't really interested in the way they answered the question of his divinity according to their friends and neighbors; he wanted to hear them answer the question for themselves.

And his intention is just as true today.

Who do you say Jesus is?

When he turns to ask you that question, is it relevant at that moment what your parents think or what your pastor thinks or what some professor of yours thinks about Jesus? No, the only thing that matters is what *you* think.

Who do *you* say Jesus is?

For while the Father has indeed ordained the Son to be "the head of the body, the church" (Col. 1:18), the church is built one person at a time as individuals are drawn into it under the conviction of the Holy Spirit. The church's victory is *assured* by the overcoming life of Christ, but its victory is *revealed* every time doubt is transformed into faith in the heart of a believer.

People's opinions about Christ come and go. The questions may be slightly different across the centuries, but all the questions in the world can be summed up in the one personal question every man and woman must ultimately answer:

Who do *you* say Jesus is?

Christ wants private conviction to become public confession. It would be a misunderstanding of Jesus' question to think that he is content for people to give a silent nod of assent to him without declaring openly their Christian faith and belief.

This is the point where many people stumble along the road to salvation. More indicatively, this is the point where many people minimize or completely do away with their need for the church. When someone says they can worship Christ in their own way or that their religion is a private matter between them and God, they are *stopping short* of Jesus' clear command and *selling short* the wonder of his Body. Jesus said, "Everyone who will acknowledge Me before men, I will also acknowledge him before My Father in heaven. But whoever denies Me before men, I will also deny him before My Father in heaven" (Matt. 10:32–33). The message is clear, and the consequences are profound.

This is why Jesus reacted so affirmingly to the response of Peter to his question. You know Simon Peter. Normally, the only time he opened his mouth was when he needed to change feet. He was always quick with an answer, even when the words made only a brief stopover at his brain for processing.

But this time he happened to get it right. Jesus had asked, "Who do you say that I am?" Peter's answer was equally bold and determined: "You are the Christ, the Son of the living God." He confessed Jesus the same way we are to confess him—outwardly, publicly, verbally, and dogmatically.

The folly of private Christianity is that it is really a veiled attempt to keep a foot on both sides of the fence—to not commit one's self entirely to the notion that Christ is Lord, to pick and choose those instances when religious faith is of most comfort and benefit.

If you know anything about the teachings of Christ, though, you know that fence-sitting is not an option in the kind of life he modeled and described. In the passage immediately following this one in Matthew 16, Jesus began revealing to his disciples the harsh realities that awaited him over the course of the next few months. Peter—this same Peter—"took Him aside and began to rebuke Him, saying, 'Far be it from You, Lord; this shall not happen to You!'" (v. 22 NKJV).

Just moments earlier, Jesus had been delighted by Peter's out-loud, in-public declaration of Christian faith. But now, notice Jesus' staggering admonishment of Peter's whispered, hushed, off-to-the-side appeal toward self-preservation: "Get behind Me, Satan!" Jesus said, "You are an offense to Me, for you are not mindful of the things of God, but the things of men" (v. 23 NKJV).

Then turning to the rest of his followers, he shared with them these serious, familiar words of surrender and submission that cut to the heart of Christian discipleship: "If anyone desires to come after Me, let him deny himself, and take up his cross, and follow Me. For whoever desires to save his life will lose it, but whoever loses his life for My sake will find it. For what profit is it to a man if he gains the whole world, and loses his own soul?" (vv. 24–26).

The church is Christ's out-in-the-open declaration of who he is and what he is doing. We who are his followers must stand together in full view of the world, willing to suffer whatever price our association with him costs us, for "what will a man give in exchange for his soul?" (v. 26).

Finally, Christ guarantees the church's perpetual victory. Jesus responded to Peter's public confession of faith with a bold promise of his own: "I say to you that you are Peter, and on this rock I will build My church, and the gates of Hades shall not prevail against it" (v. 18).

We know that the Roman Catholic Church interprets this verse as being a decree from Christ that someone from Peter's lineage will perpetually rule the church as its pope. If you'll read this verse carefully, however, you'll notice that Jesus clearly had a more substantial decree in mind.

The name "Peter" in Greek is *petros*, the masculine form of the word that means a "small stone" or a "tiny pebble." Yet the word *rock* used in this verse comes from the feminine form—*petra*—which refers to an entire *slab* of rock or even a mountain.

Not far from where I live just east of Atlanta, Georgia, stands an enormous slab of solid rock called Stone Mountain. Its bare, gray face extends hundreds of feet above the ground and for two miles horizontally from beginning to end. It is the largest exposed mass of granite in North America.

Without a doubt it is what the Greek language would call a *petra*. Capital letters. Underlined twice. Gigantic rock.

But if you go to the base of that mountain, you can easily kick up all kinds of loose gravel that has found its way there by being dislodged from the much, much larger rock. Pick up one of these little stones, stare up at the mountain it came from, and you'll have a good sense of why the rock you're holding in your hand is not best described as a *petra* but as a *petros*—a tiny pebble.

Jesus said, "You are Peter—*petros*—[a little rock], but upon this *petra*—[this big rock, this brave confession of yours about who I am and what I came to do]— I will build my church."

Any doubt about who this *petra* really is can be easily answered with another Scripture, this time from 1 Corinthians 10. There Paul is speaking to the New Testament church about the children of Israel during their exodus from Egypt and their years of wandering in the wilderness. He reminds the early believers that these forefathers of theirs "all ate the same spiritual food, and all drank the same spiritual drink. For they drank from a spiritual rock that followed them, and that rock was Christ" (1 Cor. 10:3–4).

The only man who is ever to be exalted in the church is its true leader, its true rock. And that Rock is the Lord Jesus Christ, who is the only one able to crash the gates of hell, to conclude the reign of death, and to claim the final victory over the devil.

- Jesus alone, then, is the Lord of the church, and we are to obey him completely.
- He is the Leader of the church, and we are to follow him totally.
- He is the Lover of the church, and we should adore him supremely.
- He is the Life of the church, and we can know him personally.

The Founder of our church is Jesus Christ, and he is making our church a modern-day wonder.

LET US EXPRESS
THE FAITH OF THE CHURCH

As C. S. Lewis said, Christianity is a religion "you could not have guessed." How could anyone have conceived of a God willing to come to earth, making himself "of no reputation, taking the form of a bondservant, and coming in the likeness of men . . . obedient to the point of death, even the death of the cross" (Phil. 2:7–8 NKJV)?

It is this amazing reality that sets Christianity apart. The wonder of our Lord and Savior is that he is both human and divine.

- He is so human that he could be born in a stable, yet he is so divine that angels came to announce his virgin birth.
- He is so human that he could get tired and have to lie down to get some rest while crossing the Sea of Galilee, yet he is so divine that he could speak to a storm and hush the wind and the waves.
- He is so human that he could climb into a sheltered spot on a mountainside to pray through the night, yet he is so divine that the mountain he rested against was created by his very hand.
- He is so human that he could weep at the grave of Lazarus, yet he is so divine that he could speak to Lazarus beyond the grave and raise him from the dead.
- He is so human that he could physically die after hours of sheer torture on the cross, yet he is so divine that he could come back to life— never to die again.

This is our Christian faith and belief. It is powerful enough all on its own—just as it is presented in the Scripture—to compel men and women to reach out to Christ as their Lord and Savior. Yet God in his providence has given this message to the church. He has instructed us to learn it, to live it, and to share its glories with others.

A DIVINE DELEGATION

I am amazed that God entrusted such an important task to us. I know what it's like to delegate tasks to others. I understand the amount of trust and confidence that's required in order to assign a responsibility to someone else. Many of us in leadership positions find ourselves forced to do this out of necessity and expediency. A few of us learn over time to embrace it, realizing that involving others in the work of the kingdom is a vital activity, a key component in Christ's desire that we work together and build each other up. But hardly any of us are ever totally free to look at an assignment we've entrusted to another person without thinking in the back of our minds that we could do it better ourselves—to hope against hope that they won't let us down.

So when I think of God—almighty, all-knowing, all-everything God—choosing to authorize a motley collection of people like you and me to share his life-giving gospel with the world, I just . . . I just don't know what to say. How could he possibly think that people he knows as well as he knows us could do anything but mess this up?

Yet he does it anyway—not because he trusts the church's commitment to his cause, but because he trusts what he can do through a church that's fully surrendered to him.

COMMITTED OR SURRENDERED?

Notice the not-so-subtle distinction between *commitment* and *surrender*.

When we commit ourselves to something, we promise to bring the full weight of our efforts to bear on the task we've agreed to perform. We vow to make whatever sacrifices are necessary. And though we know we won't do it perfectly, we guarantee to give it our best shot.

Commitment is based purely on ourselves and our own work.

Now let's be honest here—is that really what we want our Christian service and obedience to be dependent upon? Have we not proven to ourselves enough times by now that our faithfulness is limited by our tendency to sin? Does anyone know better than we do how easily we're distracted from the things Christ desires of us?

But what if our pledge to Christ was not *commitment* but *surrender*? What if we stopped gritting our teeth and forcing our way into others' lives and instead relinquished all the responsibility to him—to the one who really doesn't need our work gloves but only our willingness?

Isn't that sort of what Jesus was saying when, after Peter's clear confession of faith, he confirmed to him, "Blessed are you, Simon Bar-Jonah, for flesh and blood has not revealed this to you, but My Father who is in heaven" (Matt. 16:17 NKJV)? Jesus wasn't praising Peter for what he had done; he was praising the Father for what he was doing in Peter's submitted heart.

Our faith in Christ is not a matter of human reasoning; it is a matter of heavenly revelation. We don't come to him by figuring everything out; we come to him by faith. Therefore, when we share the love of God with others, though our mouths are the ones moving, the work and results of our witnessing rests squarely on the shoulders of Christ.

And, my friend, that is good news!

Only God can open the eyes of the spiritually blind. Only God can open the ears of the spiritually deaf. Only God can give life to the spiritually dead. If there is any hope—and there is lots of it!—for our churches to clearly express the Christian faith to our cities, our towns, our nation, and our world, it will not start with our commitment but with our surrender.

That's why Jesus could say to his early followers, "You will even be brought before governors and kings because of Me, to bear witness to them and to the nations. But when they hand you over, don't worry about how or what you should speak. For you will be given what to say at that hour, because you are not speaking, but the Spirit of your Father is speaking in you" (Matt. 10:18–20).

That's why Paul could reason with the early church: "Since, in God's wisdom the world did not know God through wisdom, God was pleased to save those who believe through the foolishness of the message preached" (1 Cor. 1:21).

That's why we are reminded through this "faithful saying" to put our trust in *his* work, not in our own: "If we are faithless, He remains faithful, for He cannot deny Himself" (2 Tim. 2:13).

Christ's confidence is in himself. His kingdom is in his hands. "No one can come to Me," he said, "unless the Father who sent Me draws him" (John 6:44). Clearly, he doesn't need us. Yet—wonder of wonders—he chooses to use us as we open our arms wide to whatever he wants to do through our lives.

Our churches can never be *committed* enough to him to do anything of eternal value, but our churches can be *surrendered* enough to him to turn this world upside down.

And who wouldn't like to see a little of that?

THE CHURCH UNITED

This grand hope of evangelizing the world can only materialize, however, as we unite with our brothers and sisters in the church, devoting ourselves to one another, and submitting our wills corporately to Christ.

The church—and the church alone—is his base of operations.

That's why we should be suspicious of any free-lance Christians who go off doing their own thing in isolation from the body of Christ. Those who are unwilling to align themselves with the church, who insist on their own independence, and who refuse the wisdom and protection of its authority have placed themselves outside the will of God.

The church is not perfect and doesn't claim to be. The church is not God and doesn't want to be. But the church and only the church has been delegated spiritual authority by the Lord Jesus Christ. No one who chooses to work exclusively outside of it can claim Christ's sponsorship and blessing.

When Jesus appeared to his eleven apostles just prior to his ascension, he said to them, "All authority has been given to Me in heaven and on earth. Go, therefore, and make disciples of all nations, baptizing them in the name of the Father and of the Son and of the Holy Spirit, teaching them to observe everything I have commanded you. And remember, I am with you always, to the end of the age" (Matt. 28:18–20).

These eyewitnesses of the resurrected Christ were soon to be filled with the Holy Spirit at Pentecost and dispersed throughout the known world to establish the church beyond the small pocket of Jerusalem. The Lord had not merely given this challenge to them as individuals but to the churches they would lead and grow, to the churches they would spawn and multiply, to the churches that have now crisscrossed the globe as their descendants—churches like yours and mine.

We are the heirs of this Great Commission. At times we obey this high calling one on one, as a personal responsibility we carry into every day. But unless we see ourselves as representatives of Christ and his church, we find ourselves in a dangerous place without mooring and accountability, without strength and support, without the unity of shared purpose and love that gives our witness an authentic look and feel.

This doesn't mean that there is only one way of doing things. It doesn't mean that any one person in the church can rule heavy-handedly, choking the dreams and creativity of its members, retaining in a small handful of people all that the Spirit is saying.

But it does mean that the church has a purpose beyond only getting together on Sunday morning. The church is a powerful marching force of redeemed sinners, doing together what none of us can do by ourselves—proclaiming Christ's love to the lost, receiving the saved into the fold, and discipling believers to become all that Jesus has called them to be.

And until we become OK with working in tandem with one another, embracing the sometimes difficult task of finding unity in such diversity, we will struggle to be faithful to Christ, we will have a hard time feeling good about our effectiveness, and we will flit from place to place to find our purpose—when all the while our purpose is to be a surrendered heart in God's church.

LET US BE EXCITED
ABOUT THE FUTURE OF THE CHURCH

Jesus said two things about the church that guarantees its future:

- "I will build My church."
- "And the gates of Hades shall not prevail against it."

This is the first mention of the church in the New Testament, the only prediction Jesus made about its establishment. Yet when he said "I will build My church," he gave the strongest possible promise of the church's ultimate success. He said all he really needed to say.

But notice that he didn't say, "*You* will build My church."

Neither did he say, "I will build *your* church."

His exact words were, "*I* will build *My* church."

We are not building the church for Jesus; he is building the church for himself. If it were left solely to the efforts and genius of the people of God, we would have buried the church in the ground a long time ago. Our track record throughout history proves that when we take the church into our own hands, we always make things worse.

But when God builds a house for his people, that house is built to last forever.

THE MASTER BUILDER

King David thought the best thing he could do for God was to build him a magnificent temple that would stand forever as a testimony to God's glory and greatness—a place for the people of Israel to come for generations and worship their Creator. His dream was finally realized during the reign of his son Solomon, but this awesome tribute to the wonder and faithfulness of God could not survive the aftershocks of a divided kingdom, the plundering of its treasuries by the nation's own leaders, and (finally) the gleeful fire of Nebuchadnezzar's marauding armies. It fell in 586 B.C. after standing for nearly four centuries.

But within a generation, King Cyrus of Persia permitted the Jews to return to Israel from their Babylonian exile and rebuild the temple their enemies had destroyed. Zerubbabel's Temple (as it came to be called) stood for another 350 years until the wear and tear of political unrest caused it to fall into disrepair and eventually into the hands of Antiochus, the Seleucid king, who blasphemously burned a pig on the temple altar.

For a brief time, the Maccabean revolt reclaimed and purified the temple, but the greedy reach of the Roman Empire proved too strong, and the throne of Palestine became occupied by foreigners. One of these kings, Herod, decided to please his Jewish subjects by rebuilding the temple. And though this temple formed a backdrop throughout most of the New Testament years, it proved an irresistible object lesson for the Roman emperor Titus, who leveled it in A.D. 70.

That's just the way it goes with the things we build.

Thankfully, we are not the ones who are building God's church. Jesus is the Builder. We are merely the bricks—the "living stones" that are being built into "a spiritual house for a holy priesthood to offer up spiritual sacrifices acceptable to God through Jesus Christ" (1 Pet. 2:5). He is "the Head—Christ. From Him the whole body [is] fitted and knit together" (Eph. 4:15–16).

The church is not the building where you gather for worship. The church is built on the sure foundation of Jesus Christ—himself being the chief cornerstone. And wherever believers in Christ are united together through faith in him, the church stands on his shoulders. It will never fall.

You see, Jesus and the church are not identical, but they are inseparable. So when you say that you love Jesus, you must also mean that you love his church— the church *he* loved so much that he "gave Himself for her, to make her holy, cleansing her in the washing of water by the word. He did this to present the church to Himself in splendor, without spot or wrinkle or any such thing, but holy and blameless" (Eph. 5:25–27).

Do you see what Christ has invested in the church?

Do you see the loving care he feels for it?

Do you see how dependent we are on him?

Our job, then, is simply to follow his Word, pray for his guidance, and proceed in his direction because Jesus will not take us anywhere that is not best for his kingdom and best for his church. He will build his church one way or the other—with us or without us—and we who have sometimes tried to do it without him are the first to be thankful that we are in his capable hands.

SOMEBODY BETTER WATCH OUT

But Jesus is not just the church's Builder; he is its General, leading us into a battle we are absolutely assured of winning. Jesus said that he would not only build his church but that "the gates of Hades shall not prevail against it." Even hell itself cannot stop his building program.

When you think about it, "gates" are not designed for offense. No one goes into war with gates in their weaponry. No, gates are a defensive measure, an attempt to keep the enemy out, to keep the city safe from intruders.

Therefore, we can gather from Jesus' words that it is not the mission of the church to stop hell; rather, it is the mission of hell to try stopping the church. And I use the word *try* because that's about all hell has to give. It can try, but it cannot succeed.

Hell *can* do a lot of things, of course. It can twist people's reasoning to accept the shameful slaughter of millions of lives through the crime of abortion. It can possess a madman to exterminate millions of Jews in the death chambers of the holocaust. It can tempt individuals to turn their backs on God and walk in their own sinful flesh.

But hell cannot stop the church—not even for a pivotal few moments that make you wonder if the gates will hold—not by springing a leak here and there until the church can locate a big enough opening to walk through. No, the church advances—as it has through the centuries, as it will throughout all time—and the gates just splinter off their hinges, smashed into a thousand pieces, practically lying down before the onslaught of the victorious Christ and his beloved bride.

Now, if you're not a part of the church, this victory doesn't apply to you. The gates of hell may be a poor match for the church, but they are certainly tall, wide, and strong enough to stop anyone who attempts to approach them alone. The only thing more formidable than the gates of hell are the people of God—together.

MARCH TO VICTORY

Why did Jesus choose this imagery to communicate the supremacy of the church? What is behind those "gates of Hades" that's so important?

A quick definition of terms makes it clear. The word *Hades* literally means "the abode of the dead." And it is the job of the church to storm the gates of death—spiritual death, emotional death, and personal death—to free those chained to the sin they inherited from the fall and to carry them away by God's grace to the realm of the redeemed.

These gates of death cannot prevail against the life of God the Son.

These gates of darkness cannot prevail against the light of God the Spirit.

These gates of despair cannot prevail against the love of God the Father.

Think of all the opportunities the devil has had to bring the church to its knees, all the things the church has endured throughout its two thousand years of existence—persecutions from without and problems from within.

- It has been attacked by its foes and neglected by its friends.
- It has been infected with heresies and stained with compromise.
- It has been weakened by strife and crippled by selfishness.

Yet the church is still on its feet. The gates of hell are still quivering with its every step. And death is still showing its weakness for a God-man who proved too strong to contain and for a ragtag bunch of people who now carry inside of themselves the same power the Father "demonstrated in the Messiah by raising Him from the dead and seating Him at His right hand in the heavens—far above every ruler and authority, power and dominion, and every title given, not only in this age but also in the one to come" (Eph. 1:20–21).

So, what started with Jesus on the dusty paths of Palestine grew into a crew of twelve men who followed him. By the morning of Pentecost, that group of followers numbered 120 people, and by the end of that day the church had reached what (to them) must have seemed the astronomical amount of 3,000 souls.

In A.D. 45—roughly ten years after Christ's resurrection—there were 100,000 people who called themselves Christians. By A.D. 300 the number was 12 million. By A.D. 1000—50 million. By A.D. 1500—100 million.

And the wave of growth was just beginning. In 1800, more than 200 million Christians lived on the earth. In 1900, the church totaled more than 500 million. Today the number of believers on the planet is an estimated 1.9 billion—that's *billion* with a *b*. In fact, more people came to Christ in the twentieth century than in the first nineteen centuries of the church *combined!*

How do you explain that?

Jesus said, "I will build My church." That's how.

It's really "wonderful" when you think about it, isn't it?

BUILT TO LAST

I read a story about a man who hired a carpenter to build a fence. He said to the carpenter, "I want you to build a fence four feet high. But I want you not only to guarantee me that it will be four feet high; I want you to guarantee me that it will never fall." So after thinking through some possible solutions for a few days, the carpenter called the man and said, "I'm going to build your fence, and I'll let you know when it's finished."

One day the man got another phone call from the carpenter, who said, "I'm ready to collect my money."

The man responded, "Is the fence four feet high?"

"Yes, to the inch."

"Will it fall down?" the man asked.

"It is absolutely impossible for this fence to ever fall down," the carpenter replied.

"How can you assure me of that?"

The carpenter answered, "Well, I not only built it four feet high, I also built it five feet thick so that if it does fall down it will still be a foot higher than it was before it fell."

The church is the castle of our King, the Lord Jesus Christ. It is the only institution on earth guaranteed to last until the end of time. There is a difference between walking into a church, getting inside of a church, and being in the church. The King who is building his castle on the outside wants you to be a part of his people on the inside. What a privilege to be a part of what Jesus Christ himself is building!

CHAPTER 5

THE KING
AND I

Living a Personally Blessed Life

1941.

You don't have to be in your sixties to know the most memorable event of that year. Even the calendar date is common knowledge: December 7—the bombing of Pearl Harbor.

1963.

If you were more than two or three years old on November 22, 1963, you remember where you were when you first heard the news that President John F. Kennedy had been shot in Dallas, Texas.

2001.

It's a date so near to our own—with so many of its events and happenings still fresh in our memories—we haven't yet gotten used to a year in our decade having historical significance. But mention the numbers 9-11, and each of us can recall a memory that stands ominously above all the others.

The prophet Isaiah had a memorable date like that in his life. We could probably figure out its exact calendar date B.C. if we'd put a pencil to it, but there's something in the way Isaiah recorded it that resonates with our hearts a lot more quickly than any ordinary number would.

He simply called it "the year that King Uzziah died" (Isa. 6:1).

In the Jewish culture of that day, "the year that King Uzziah died" had far-reaching implications for everyone. This man had been king over Judah (the southern half of the divided kingdom) for more than fifty years—for as long as many people had been alive—certainly Isaiah. Uzziah had primarily reigned during a period of great material prosperity in the land. He had mounted a successful campaign against the Philistines, had established secure trading routes throughout the region, and had refortified the walls of Jerusalem with protective add-ons and towers.

Because of a rash indiscretion of his—of thinking his kingly title also gave him the right to preside in the role of priest over his people (as kings in many of the neighboring nations did)—God struck him down with leprosy until the day of his death. Yet no one could argue with the fact that, for the most part, life under Uzziah's reign had been good, the land had been at peace, and the people had felt a relative sense of safety.

But now King Uzziah—the only king many of his subjects had ever known—was dead. It seemed almost impossible to think of anyone else ruling from his throne. But if you were to ask Isaiah about the main thing that happened to him "the year that King Uzziah died"—though he, too, shared the same deep emotions of disbelief as his fellow countrymen—he'd have only one thing to say: "In the year that King Uzziah died, I saw the Lord sitting on a throne, high and lifted up, and the train of His robe filled the temple" (Isa. 6:1).

You see, Isaiah had come face to face with the King of kings and the Lord of lords. He knew the date, he knew the place, he knew the time, he knew the weather conditions.

And he never forgot it.

Above [the temple] stood seraphim; each one had six wings: with two he covered his face, with two he covered his feet, and with two he flew. And one cried to another and said:
    "Holy, holy, holy is the LORD of hosts;
    the whole earth is full of His glory!"
And the posts of the door were shaken by the voice of him who cried out, and the house was filled with smoke.
    So I said:
    "Woe is me, for I am undone!
    Because I am a man of unclean lips,
    And I dwell in the midst of a people of unclean lips;
    For my eyes have seen the King,
    the LORD of hosts." (Isa. 6:2–5)

Now *that's* a vision from God!

A FRESH VISION

Isaiah knew this was no ordinary walk in the park. He had seen God! He had seen his glory! He had seen something not everyone is open enough to the ways of God to experience!

But I'm telling you, what we all need today is a fresh vision of almighty God. Our nation needs it. Our churches need it. You need it. I need it. For until our lives become characterized as "the King and I in a personal, ongoing, developing relationship"—not as "the King and what I've heard about him" or "the King and what my parents always believed about him"—we will not know either the depths of Isaiah's surrender or the heights of Isaiah's faithfulness and effectiveness.

I know that this talk about "visions" scares some people. I'm not speaking about some kind of out-of-body experience or a weird warp in time and space. I'm talking about falling in such deep love with Jesus, becoming so focused on his kingdom, and recapturing such a wonder for the potential of his church that every fiber of our being longs to know Christ better, to hear what he is saying, and to obey him without hesitation.

When we do that, things will start happening in our lives that are not normal. That's not to say that they're creepy or extraterrestrial. Not at all. They're just not normal the way *normal* is defined by one who is serving God out of a mechanical, methodical, lifeless expression of Christianity.

Life under the lordship of Christ is exuberant and exciting. Sure, it's often filled with risks and dangers to our comfort zones, but it explodes with opportunities to serve and to grow. It's a daily adventure in the Master's service, complete with more joyful, unexpected experiences in a year than some people enjoy in a lifetime.

But it all starts with seeing God in a fresh, new way—looking at God through eyes like Isaiah's, willing to do whatever he asks, willing to follow him no matter how much it costs. Like Isaiah, there are several things we can do so that *The King and I* will be more than the title of an award-winning Broadway play. It will be the description of an unbelievable relationship between you and the King of kings.

STEP 1: CONTEMPLATE THE HOLINESS OF THE KING

Do you remember a time when you shook hands with someone important? Maybe it was a professional athlete or a television celebrity or the governor of your state. Even while you were standing in line or waiting to be seen, your heart was beating fast, you were rehearsing the words you might say, and you felt in your stomach the pins and needles of nervousness.

We feel that way because we're not accustomed to being in the presence of greatness. We live most of our days in an ordinary fashion, relating to people we know by first name, doing the familiar tasks that comprise the normal routine of our lives. But to see someone we've long admired, someone we've watched on the news or at the movies, someone who regularly rubs shoulders with the rich and famous, is a thrill we can feel down into the soles of our shoes.

I want you to know that when you greet God in the morning after a good night's sleep, you are meeting someone who is more than just "important." You are meeting with someone so important that his sacred name, Yahweh, was deemed too holy to even speak aloud by the early Jews, lest they mispronounce it. You are meeting with someone who existed before time and created all there is. You are meeting with the one who sets up heads of government and who rules over the affairs of men in accordance with his holy will.

This is almighty God you're addressing. Don't take this privilege lightly.

Isaiah didn't.

Mouth agape, he watched in stunned silence as the Lord appeared on his throne, encircled by the awesome sight of seraphim—"flaming ones"—who cried aloud to one another, "Holy, holy, holy is the LORD of hosts; the whole earth is full of His glory."

HOLY, HOLY, HOLY

Let's first establish who Isaiah was seeing on the throne. The apostle John makes this clear in his Gospel when he speaks about those who were not accepting the message of who Christ was. John quotes the prophet's words from Isaiah 6, which foretold that many people would see Jesus with their eyes but not believe on him with their hearts. Then John summarizes the passage by announcing, "Isaiah said these things because he saw His glory and spoke about Him" (John 12:41).

The Lord seated on his throne in the Old Testament, then, was none other than the Jesus we see in the New Testament—the Lord Jesus Christ.

And what were the words the angels were repeating in Jesus' presence?

"Holy, holy, holy!"

Seven out of every twelve references to the name of God in the Old Testament refer to him with the adjective *holy*—that's more often than any of the other descriptions of him put together! So if you've ever wondered what the chief attribute of God is, you can find it along with Isaiah at the base of God's throne, with the King "high and lifted up," the aura of his glory clouding the whole scene in wonder.

Above all else—he is holy.

- The chief attribute of God is not his virtual *power*. The seraphim were not shouting, "Omnipotent! Omnipotent! Omnipotent is the Lord of hosts!"
- The chief attribute of God is not his visual *perception*. The seraphim were not shouting, "Omniscient! Omniscient! Omniscient is the Lord of hosts!"
- The chief attribute of God is not his visible *presence*. The seraphim were not shouting, "Omnipresent! Omnipresent! Omnipresent is the Lord of hosts!"

When the angels looked at God, they just saw "holy, holy, holy!"

The main tool for creating emphasis in Hebrew poetry is the element of repetition. In the same way that we might underline or italicize a word, perhaps put it in boldface type or stamp it with an exclamation point, the Jewish writer often repeated a word for good measure. To repeat it *three* times indicated that the writer was elevating that word to its highest level of importance.

Only one attribute of God is lifted to such a superlative degree in the Bible. Only one of his countless character traits is treated to such heights of honor.

- As big as God's heart is, the Bible never says that he is "love, love, love."

- As sweet as God's grace is, the Bible never says that he is "mercy, mercy, mercy."
- As true as God's fairness is, the Bible never says that he is "justice, justice, justice."

But it does say that he is "holy, holy, holy."

This holiness is not something he possesses; it is something he *is*. "No one is holy like the LORD, for there is none besides You, nor is there any rock like our God" (1 Sam. 2:2). We praise him, we worship him, we exalt him—not because we feel like it, not because he's done some really nice things for us, not because he needs it. We "exalt the LORD our God, and worship at His footstool—for He is holy" (Ps. 99:5).

That one reason is more than enough.

That's why those who can casually settle for calling him the "good Lord" or "the man upstairs" or some nebulous "higher power" with no real name or identity do not really know the God of Scripture.

More than anything else, the God of the Bible is holy. And we who are his are wholly in his care.

GOD IS IN CONTROL

As I've mentioned, these were troubling days for Isaiah and the nation of Judah. When Isaiah caught his vision of God seated high on his heavenly throne, he was seeing God in the context of a now-empty earthly throne. The seat of authority that Uzziah had occupied for five decades sat vacant. The stability he had represented in the eyes of his people was now being shattered by the approaching armies of the north and the real awareness that the national outlook was bleak. Yet while the throne in Judah was empty, God was showing Isaiah that the throne in heaven was full.

Uzziah had been shown to be mortal, but the heavenly King was immortal. One king had died—as all kings do—but one King lives forever as no other king can.

Even in our day—with the threats of terrorist attacks and smallpox epidemics, with militant homosexuality and cultural dissipation, with increasing persecution and spiritual hostility—God appears to us through the pages of his Word to remind us that he is on the throne.

When the plane hits the tower, God is in control.

When the doctor says you have cancer, God is in control.

When the boss says, "You're fired!"—God is in control.

No matter what we face in life, our holy God has already measured its impact, has already restrained it from being more than we can bear, and has already transformed it into a testimony to his glory.

Never fear. God is in control.

STEP 2: CONFESS YOUR SINFULNESS TO THE KING

No sooner had Isaiah seen this awesome display of God's holiness than his hands went up to shield his face, tears of shame filled his eyes, and—almost before he knew what he was saying—he burst out with the words,

"Woe is me, for I am undone!

Because I am a man of unclean lips,

And I dwell in the midst of a people of unclean lips;

For my eyes have seen the King, the LORD of hosts."

(Isa. 6:5)

When Isaiah saw the Lord in his holiness, he saw himself in his sinfulness.

When Isaiah saw the Lord in his holiness, he saw himself in his hellishness.

When Isaiah saw the Lord in his holiness, he saw himself for who he really was.

If you were to have asked people on the street what they thought of Isaiah, they'd have told you he was a man of unquestioned integrity and moral righteousness, - the epitome of personal holiness and a paragon of virtue.

If you were to have asked Isaiah (before this encounter, at least) what he thought of *himself,* he'd have probably shifted his feet a little, ducked his head in customary humility, and told you . . . well . . . he wasn't perfect by any means, but he figured he was a pretty good old fellow.

After just one glance at the holy God, however, Isaiah came clean with his filthiness. It took deity to reveal his dirtiness. It took God to reveal his guilt.

And it will always be the same with us.

BALD-FACED LIVES

Without a clear picture of who God is, our picture of who we are is a portrait of deception. It's a picture so carefully drawn—with just the right features put in and just the right features left out—that it can easily fool the people who see us from a distance. It can many times fool the people who see us from up close. And believe it or not, it can even fool the person who drew the picture to begin with.

That's how out-of-reality our self-perceptions can be when we're weighing them against the shifting tide of cultural morality or when using nothing more than apples-and-oranges comparisons with other people. Jeremiah certainly knew what he was talking about when he said, "The heart is deceitful above all things, and desperately wicked; who can know it?" (Jer. 17:9).

But the closer we get to God—the more time we spend in his presence—the sooner the bright colors we use for our personal portrait begin to darken into a hideous black. It is only by the substituted righteousness of Christ being applied to our lives that we are able to do anything about it.

You certainly see this happening in the life of Paul. I'm sure he thought he was making a bold statement concerning his needy position before God when he wrote in 1 Corinthians 15:9, "I am the least of the apostles."

But notice the slightly different comparison after seven more years as a Christian believer, when Paul said he was "the least of all the saints" (Eph. 3:8).

Three years later, his opinion of his personal righteousness wasn't even in the same class as the apostles and the other saints of God. As he wrote to Timothy: "This saying is trustworthy and deserving of full acceptance: 'Christ Jesus came into the world to save sinners'—and I am the worst of them" (1 Tim. 1:15).

Does this man who's growing lower every day in his own estimation of himself sound like someone who's growing in Christ? You'd better believe he does! The nearer we get to God's holiness, the more our tiniest sins take on disheartening proportions. The closer we get to God's heart, the quicker we want to return to him in repentance, to throw ourselves on the wide expanse of his mercy. Those who view us from the *outside* are in all likelihood seeing someone who is growing in grace, bearing the fruit of the Spirit, and becoming more like Christ in attitude and action—which is true. But from where we stand on the *inside*, we realize more each day that any righteous behavior of ours is a gift from God, not something for which we can take any credit.

THE TROUBLE WITH ME

Many years ago, *The Times* of London ran a series of letters to the editor on the subject, "What is wrong with the world?" As you can imagine, this topic stimulated great interest for a long period of time, generating opinions from readers all over the world. Some of the views came from well-known and highly respected members of society, all intent on answering the unanswerable question of what makes the world a difficult place in which to live.

One day a letter arrived from the great Christian philosopher and author G. K. Chesterton. His entry was brief and to the point:

> To the Editor,
> *The Times* of London
> Dear Sir,
> You ask what is wrong with the world—I am.

And with that, the case was closed. Everyone realized that he had hit the nail on the head.

This same feeling was Isaiah's conclusion after seeing the holiness of God in its purest form. The problems facing his nation were not God's fault. They were not their enemies' fault. Their problems were *their* fault. In a very personal, responsible sense, they were *Isaiah's* fault. Until we come to this point in our relationship with Christ, we will continue to find someone else to blame for the troubles in our lives. The stubborn bullies of our selfish natures will continue to frustrate our best efforts at submitting to him, and we will sputter along in fits and starts in our Christian walk, unable to string together what a great writer of the past once called "a long obedience in one direction."

The problem is our sin.

But the news gets better. God has an answer.

> One of the seraphim flew to me, having in his hand a live coal which he had taken with the tongs from the altar. And he touched my mouth with it, and said:
> "Behold, this has touched your lips;
> Your iniquity is taken away,
> And your sin purged." (Isa. 6:6–7)

Boy, does that feel better—not that it required such a precious sacrifice from God's throne to pay the penalty we owed on our sin, not that the price of Christian faith is the burning away of our old flesh—but that God has supplied a remedy.

He didn't have to.

But our holy God is also a God of mercy. That's why time after time in the Scripture—and day after day in cities and towns like yours—God springs into action as people confess their sins and receive from him the healing touch of full forgiveness. "If we confess our sins, He is faithful and righteous to forgive us our sins and to cleanse us from all unrighteousness" (1 John 1:9).

If people are not saved, it's not because God has made the way to himself too difficult. Those who persist in their unbelief, who continue to put even the slightest amount of stock in their own goodness and dignity, remain outside God's grace because they don't think they really need it.

But we know better, don't we? Like Isaiah, we know it will hurt at some level to have the hot coals of God's holiness singe away the tough exterior of our pride, but it will result in the incomparable gift of a new, redeemed, forgiven heart.

Bring on the burning.

STEP 3: COMMIT TO THE USEFULNESS OF THE KING

If the story ended here, it would be terribly depressing. Like Paul said, "If Christ has not been risen, your faith is worthless; you are still in your sins . . . [and] we should be pitied more than anyone" (1 Cor. 15:17, 19). If we were simply another in a long line of Isaiahs whose best works had again been shown to be pointless in the light of God's holiness, we'd be fairly justified in collapsing into a heap and letting life go on without us.

But the story doesn't end here. Just as God has entrusted the message of his gospel to the church— assigning holy work to people who still have a good bit of holiness to work out in their own lives—he entrusts each one of us with particular parts of his business plan.

And again, I can hardly believe such generosity.

But we're back to the point of *commitment* versus *surrender.* When God chooses to use us in his service, it's not because he's seen something in us that's worthy of being tapped for his purposes. It's not because he needs a guy with our credentials working for him.

What he sees is his own holiness . . . and a few clean vessels that are willing to let his love pour *into* and *out* of them at the bidding of the Master.

CLEAN VESSELS

I have always loved the passage in 2 Corinthians where Paul illustrates this so well: "For we do not preach ourselves, but Christ Jesus the Lord, and ourselves your bondservants for Jesus' sake. For it is the God who commanded the light to shine out of darkness, who has shone in our hearts to give the light of the knowledge of the glory of God in the face of Jesus Christ. But we have this treasure in earthen vessels, that the excellence of the power may be of God and not of us" (2 Cor. 4:5–7 NKJV).

Until we have lowered the assessment of our own value to the level of an "earthen vessel," we can be of little or no use to the Father. But once we have believed what God has revealed to us about who we really are without him, there is no limit to what he can do through us. A vessel that's considered intact and invaluable on the outside but dirty on the inside is of no value to him. But even a broken vessel—if it's been scrubbed clean by God's grace—can be put into a place of his choosing and used to refresh all who come near.

So Isaiah's humiliated pride is not the end of his life's story, as it might have been if God had just been trying to pull rank on his subjects. No—God's loving, merciful desire is to get his people where he can equip and use them. Thus, when we come to the end of ourselves, we arrive at a whole new beginning.

You see, after the confession comes the cleansing. And after the cleansing comes the calling.

HERE AM I

Let's hear Isaiah tell it:

I heard the voice of the Lord, saying,
"Whom shall I send,
And who will go for Us?"
Then I said, "Here am I! Send me." (Isa. 6:8)

"Here am I."

- Not "there he is, send him."
- Not "here am I, but send the pastor."
- Not "here am I, but send the missionary."
- Not "here am I, but send the seminary-trained professional."
- Not even "here am I, but send anyone else."

Isaiah said it the only way someone can honestly say it when they've seen God's holiness and been sickened at their own sinfulness: "Here am I, Lord. Send me."

Notice also that he didn't say, "Here *I am!*" There's a big difference between the two. Had he simply said, "Here I am," that would have simply indicated his location. But Isaiah's "here am I" revealed that he was seeking a *vocation*. He wasn't saying, "I'm right here if you need me, God. If you're going to be in the area sometime, be sure to give me a call." Instead, he was saying, "Here am I, Lord. You can move me anywhere you want to take me, or you can leave me right here where people already know me. But no matter where you place me, God, I want you to know that I'm all ears, I'm all yours, and I'm all ready. You say when, and I'll be there."

That's the heart of a man who has seen a fresh vision of God. That's the heart of a woman who has contemplated the holiness of the King. That's the heart of a student, child, or teenager who has confessed their sinfulness to the Lord.

That's a heart that will make a difference in this world.

WHAT ABOUT ME?

Some people would argue that this kind of selfless surrender is no way to chart your path through life. How could anyone, they might say, find their personal destiny by putting it all in someone else's hands?

Those who are in a little closer proximity to the church, who know how to phrase their objections with the right kind of spiritual terminology, might put it this way: "I do believe we should love God and strive to do what's right, but I've seen people who take their faith too far. They've become too heavenly minded to be of any earthly good."

If we are honest with ourselves, we will see that our opinions are sometimes similar. Hearing temptation talk in our own heads, we know what it's like to think, *I know God demands my total surrender, but I don't see how that will leave me time to take care of all the things that are important to me and my family. I mean, I'm ultimately responsible for them and for myself. I can't just quit work or be away from home every night doing God's business, can I?*

Good questions. But let me put it to you this way: The only path to a personally blessed life (and I use the word *only* very deliberately) is through full submission to Christ's lordship. You can try another way, but I can guarantee its failure.

How can I say these things and really mean them?
Jesus did:

"This is why I tell you: Don't worry about
your life, what you will eat or what you will
drink; or about your body, what you will
wear. Isn't life more than food and the body
more than clothing? Look at the birds of the
sky: they don't sow or reap or gather into
barns, yet your heavenly Father feeds them.
Aren't you worth more than they? Can any of
you add a single cubit to his height by worrying? And why do you worry about clothes?
Learn how the wildflowers of the field grow:
they don't labor or spin thread. Yet I tell you
that not even Solomon in all his splendor was
adorned like one of these! If that's how God
clothes the grass of the field, which is here
today and thrown into the furnace tomorrow,
won't he do much more for you—you of little
faith? So don't worry, saying, 'What will we
eat?' or 'What will we drink?' or 'What will
we wear?' For the Gentiles eagerly seek all
these things, and your heavenly Father knows
that you need them. But seek first the kingdom of God and His righteousness, and . . .
[and what?] . . . and all these things will be
provided for you." (Matt. 6:25–33)

Throughout this book we have discussed the things
that matter most to Christ:

- We know his rightful place of authority is important to him.
- We know that his kingdom is important to him.
- We know that his church is important to him.

Now from this extended passage of Scripture, it's hard to miss the fact that something else is of great value to him, as well:

You are.

Do you have any doubt that—when all is said and done—he will make sure that his position of absolute authority will be clearly expressed and established? Do you have any doubt that he will make sure his kingdom comes and finds its fullness in eternity? Do you have any doubt that he will build his church so strong that the gates of hell cannot resist it? So should you have any doubt that he will make sure "all these things" are "provided for you" as you seek him with all your heart?

The truth is, our doubts *do* start to build as we work down through this list. *His lordship?* Sure. *His kingdom?* Of course. *His church?* I hope so. *But me?* Well, I'm not so sure.

The Lord Jesus doesn't see things that way. Everything on his list of importance is equally as certain of being fulfilled, from his highest rule in heaven to our deepest needs on earth.

So we can quit worrying about ourselves. That's God's business. We can begin putting all our nest eggs in the basket of Christ's lordship, knowing that he will always do what's best for his kingdom, what's best for his church, and what's best for us.

It's the only way.

GO AND TELL

A godless king lay dying on the battlefield. With the clink and clash of armies and weapons still resonating off the hillsides, his swordbearer bent low to hear the final, whispered request of his fallen leader. The king spoke in resigned, somber tones: "Servant? Go and tell the dead that the king is coming."

Immediately, without thought for his own life, the servant whisked his own sword from its scabbard and thrust it into his own heart—that he might go into the world of the dead to announce the coming of the king.

I realize this story is a little gross . . . and very pagan. Yet its message is relevant to those of us who are alive at this moment in history, who have seen the King, and who have surrendered ourselves to him. Our job now is to go to the dead of this world and announce his coming.

You may not notice them right away, but God will point them out. They may look anything *but* dead in their business suits and sports cars, in their jogging pants and minivans. They may appear anything *but* needy on their landscaped decks and in their backyard pools, in their paneled dens with their big-screen TVs. They may sound anything *but* insecure by the way they talk in public. But those who are trying to maneuver through life without the benefit of Christ's forgiveness are not going to get out of here alive. Time is running out, and it will be too late before they know it.

But the King and you can do something about it. As he said to Isaiah—who had asked God for a job to do— you can "go and tell this people" about the grace of Jesus Christ. You can "go and tell this people" that life will continue to be an endless track of false starts and dead ends until Christ has cleared the path of sin from their hearts. You can "go and tell this people" that peace, hope, and joy are available without measure from the loving hands of God.

You can be of more use to the King than you ever imagined.

CROWN HIM, CROWN HIM

We in America live in what is commonly known as a democracy. (This is really a misnomer. We live in a republic, governed by the rule of law as found in the Constitution.) Still, the concept of kings, monarchies, subjects, and royalty is foreign to most of us. In fact, when many of the colonists wanted to make George Washington king, he wisely refused—not only because he felt this was not the best form of political government, but because (I suspect) he also knew there was only one King!

Yet from time immemorial, monarchy has been one of the predominant forms of government around the world. Kings, therefore, were aplenty in the culture of the Middle East where the Bible was written. One of the forms this took in the ancient Middle East was through the position of *suzerains*—sovereign monarchs over a land or territory. Their authority was absolute and unquestioned. The people were totally subject to their every command; hence, kingdom citizens were referred to as *subjects*.

There was no two-party system or bipartisan co-operation necessary in this kind of arrangement because there was only one side to any issue that really mattered—the king's! The land was ruled by his sovereignly imposed law. There was no negotiated agreement between equal parties. The king bound his subjects to himself. In effect, he *owned* them. But in return the king promised to protect, defend, and provide for the needs of his people.

The Lord Jesus Christ is our suzerain king. We are his subjects. His desire is always to do what is best for his kingdom. That is why each day of our lives we must crown him King afresh. When we do, we become kingdom-minded. Then we are truly in the driver's seat.

Why?

- Because whatever the King desires is best for the kingdom.
- Whatever is best for the kingdom is best for the church.
- And whatever is best for the church will be best for me.

It is my prayer that we, his subjects, will crown him King moment by moment so that with his power and by his grace we can get on with kingdom business!

DEVOTIONS GUIDE

I've included this two-week devotional guide to help you anchor the truths of this book into your life. The format is very simple: read a selected passage of Scripture, focus on a key verse, then spend some time dealing with a few open-ended questions.

My hope is that you will come away from this experience with a renewed heart and mind, that your first reflex of the day will be one of submission to Christ's lordship, and that you and your church will begin to experience the thrilling possibilities that arise from putting all your plans at the feet of Jesus.

In fact, these short Bible studies might be ideal for small groups in your church, where you can deal with these discussion questions in the context of your shared ministry.

In whatever way you choose to use them, I pray that these devotions will help you live in the afterglow of what we've learned together . . . and watch for the things God wants to do in and through you as a result.

May the Lord bless you as you *Crown Him King*.

1 The King and His Throne (part 1)
His Lordship Determines Our Spiritual Relationship

Bible Study: Read John 13:1–17
"You call Me Teacher and Lord.
This is well said, for so I am." (John 13:13)

1. Jesus said, "If I don't wash you, you have no part with Me" (v. 8). Consider how filthy you were before Christ cleaned you up? Consider where sin might have taken you if he hadn't loved you so much?

2. "One who has bathed doesn't need to wash anything except his feet" (v. 10). We'll always have little things to be working on, but are you able to relax in the fact that your cleanliness is already accomplished?

3. "If you know these things, you are blessed if you do them" (v. 17). Think through some of the blessings of obedience. Go deeper than usual. Ask yourself why you ever pass up these blessings.

2 The King and His Throne (part 2)
His Lordship Defines Our Personal Ownership

Bible Study: Read Isaiah 45:18–25
"For I am God, and there is no other." (Isa. 45:22)

1. Some people see life on earth as a pointless experience of randomness and chance. What ideas or evidence could you point to in order to say that God "did not create it in vain" (v. 18)?

2. And to those who might say that we "seek [God] in vain" (v. 19), how would you explain the real-world blessings and benefits of being a child of God, a servant of the Most High?

3. "Every knee shall bow, every tongue shall take an oath" (v. 23). If everyone will ultimately see Christ's lordship clearly, what is it that clouds our view of his authority in the meantime?

3 The King and His Throne (part 3)
His Lordship Demands Our Daily Stewardship

Bible Study: Read 2 Corinthians 9:6–15
"Each person should do as he has decided in his heart—not out of regret." (2 Cor. 9:7)

1. "The person who sows sparingly will also reap sparingly, and the person who sows generously will also reap generously" (v. 6). What would generous sowing look like in your life? What about the generous harvest?

2. When God says in the context of our personal stewardship that "He has scattered; He has given to the poor" (v. 9), doesn't it show how highly he values our participation in his kingdom?

3. Time. Money. They are merely tools—opportunities given to us to meet needs and to glorify God. When others look at what you do with your time or your money, what or who do they see?

4 The King and His Throne (part 4)
His Lordship Decides Our Eternal Fellowship

Bible Study: Read 1 Thessalonians 4:13–18
"And so we will always be with the Lord."
(1 Thess. 4:17)

1. In speaking about the certainty of Christ's return, Paul distinguishes believers from those "who have no hope" (v. 13). Hope is one of the exclusive properties of Christianity. What are some others?

2. "The Lord Himself" is coming for us (v. 16)— not a stranger but a friend. When we see him, we will recognize him, for his Spirit has been living in us all the while. Imagine that moment!

3. This foretelling of Christ's coming was given so we could "encourage one another with these words" (v. 18). Is that the way it feels—encouraging? Or does it kind of scare you? Do you wish he'd wait?

5 The King and His Kingdom (part 1)
We Must See the Reality of the Kingdom

Bible Study: Read Matthew 20:1–16
"So the last will be first, and the first last."
(Matt. 20:16)

1. "The kingdom of heaven is like . . ." (v. 1). If Jesus said it once, he said it a hundred times. But there is no one way to define the kingdom. What would you say "the kingdom of heaven is like"?

2. In this parable, at "noon and at three [the landowner] went out" (v. 5), just as he had done at nine and would do again at five. Describe the results of an active King.

3. "Don't I have the right to do what I want with my business?" (v. 15). When was the last time the reality of the kingdom bothered you? And when was the last time it simply blew you away?

6 The King and His Kingdom (part 2)
We Must Seek the Rule of the Kingdom

Bible Study: Read Micah 4:1–12
"The LORD will reign over them in Mount Zion
From now on, even forever." (Mic. 4:7)

1. "They shall beat their swords into plowshares" (v. 3). We're familiar with those words, but why does the kingdom's rule bring peace in its wake? And in what ways does it also cause conflict?

2. "And no one shall make them afraid" (v. 4). Is there anything about the King's rule that frightens you? Is there anything about the opponents of the kingdom that frightens you? Should it?

3. Many times in our service to the King, we will appear down for the count, as his people do in verses 9–11. Are you down right now? Have you been down before . . . and had him pull you up (v. 12)?

7 The King and His Kingdom (part 3)
We Must Show the Righteousness of the Kingdom

Bible Study: Read Colossians 3:1–17
"Let the word of Christ dwell in you richly."
(Col. 3:16)

1. "Set your minds on what is above" (v. 2). If we only knew how temporary this life really is—and what a small, imperceptible fraction it is of our eternity. How could you start thinking more that way?

2. We "have put on the new man" (v. 10). But sometimes we forget where we've put him. Sometimes we like the way the old man fits. Check yourself right now. Which clothes are you wearing?

3. Often our daily choices are simply between different shades of goodness. When you're not sure, "put on love" (v. 14). What difference could love make in a decision you're facing right now?

8 The King and His Kingdom (part 4)
We Must Share the Ruler of the Kingdom

Bible Study: Read 1 Peter 3:8–22
"Always be ready to give a defense to everyone who asks you." (1 Pet. 3:15)

1. One of the items most commonly missing in our witnessing is this: we aren't really "compassionate for one another" (v. 8). Doesn't sharing the gospel start with caring for the lost?

2. "Do not fear what they fear or be disturbed" (v. 14). Witnessing for Christ becomes as natural as talking about anything else when we just get in the habit of it. What's stopping you from starting?

3. Let this fact free you to share your Lord and Savior: he is "at God's right hand, with angels, authorities, and powers subjected to Him" (v. 22). Can such power leave us powerless?

9 The King and His Castle (part 1)
Let Us Exalt the Founder of the Church

Bible Study: Read Colossians 1:15–23
"He is also the head of the body, the church;
He is the beginning." (Col. 1:18)

1. We have not only been created by him or through him but "for Him" (v. 16). He wants us as his own. He desires us in his service. Ask yourself: Does your church want Christ as badly as he wants you?

2. It is a "mystery," all right—why Christ would choose to dwell in us, to be our "hope of glory" (v. 27). Do we really have to understand everything in order to seek his kingdom's rule in our churches?

3. Our Lord is not just exalted by our songs and prayers but also when people are taught and discipled to be "mature in Christ Jesus" (v. 28). What else constitutes lifting up Jesus in your church?

10 *The King and His Castle (part 2)*
Let Us Express the Faith of the Church

Bible Study: Read 1 Corinthians 2:1–16
"We speak God's hidden wisdom in a mystery."
(1 Cor. 2:7)

1. We're used to the pastor doing all the talking—the truly gifted explaining God's gift. But Paul deliberately avoided using "persuasive words of human wisdom" (v. 4). Can you work without them too?

2. Look at the Holy Spirit's work in verses 10–12: searching, revealing, giving, imparting. Do you realize how hard he's working in you and your church right now? How do you get in on some of that?

3. Sharing and living our Christian faith as a church is not always easy, but it's amazing how it starts to happen when "we have the mind of Christ" (v. 16). How could your church do that even better?

11 *The King and His Castle (part 3)*
Let Us Be Excited about the Future of the Church

Bible Study: Read Revelation 22:6–17
"Look, I am coming quickly,
and My reward is with Me." (Rev. 22:12)

1. When John grasped the depth of what Christ's return would mean, he "fell down to worship" (v. 8). How do we reignite that kind of expectation, that kind of passion, that kind of joy?

2.   "I am the Alpha and the Omega, the First and the Last, the Beginning and the End" (v. 13). Does the certainty of our King's victory cause us to rest on our laurels—or to work out our salvation?

3.   "The one who is thirsty should come" (v. 17)—no matter what they look like, no matter what their background, no matter how many times they've said these same words before. How well does your church do that?

12 The King and I (part 1)
Contemplate the Holiness of the King

Bible Study: Read Hebrews 12:14–29
"Serve God acceptably, with reverence and awe."
(Heb. 12:28)

1.   Even Moses, looking into the eyes of God, was "terrified and trembling" (v. 21). If a great big Bible guy like Moses could get weak in the knees at the sight of God, then what about us?

2.   God may not seem as scary as he did at Mt. Sinai, but "if they did not escape when they rejected Him who warned them on earth, even less will we if we turn away from Him who warns us from heaven" (v. 25).

3.   Although the way has been cleared by Christ for us to be comfortable in God's presence, we must never forget that "our God is a consuming fire" (v. 29). How valuable is healthy fear in your life?

13 The King and I (part 2)
Confess Your Sinfulness to the King

Bible Study: Read Hebrews 10:19–39
"Let us draw near with a true heart."
(Heb. 10:22)

1. Among the sweetest blessings of salvation is that we can experience "our hearts sprinkled clean from an evil conscience and our bodies washed in pure water" (v. 22). Is anything more refreshing than that?

2. One of the greatest weapons in our fight against sin is assembling ourselves together and "exhorting one another" (v. 25) to courage in our daily struggles. Are you doing that—and being that for others?

3. Our race through life is a long-distance marathon. We must daily depend on God's grace, that we might not be of "those who draw back . . . but those who have faith" (v. 39). Run today's leg bravely.

14 The King and I (part 3)
Commit to the Usefulness of the King

Bible Study: Read Ephesians 4:1–16
"Walk worthy of the calling you have received."
(Eph. 4:1)

1. We're all at different places in our Christian walk, so it's important that we're concentrating on our own devotion and "accepting one another in love" (v. 2). How could you do that better?

2. Do you ever feel "tossed . . . and blown" (v. 14), erratically serving Christ and not so sure what you believe? What do verses 11–15 offer as antidotes to or protections against this kind of life experience?

3. Your usefulness may not look like everyone else's. That's OK. The church works best, not when everyone is worn out but "by the proper working of each individual part" (v. 16). Do you know what your work is?